Phenomenal fat quarter quilts

new Projects with Tips to Inspire & Enhance Your Quiltmaking

M'Liss Rae Hawley

C&T PUBLISHING

Text © 2004 M'Liss Rae Hawley
Artwork © 2004 C&T Publishing, Inc.
Publisher: Amy Marson
Editorial Director: Gailen Runge
Acquisitions Editor: Jan Grigsby
Editor: Darra Williamson
Technical Editors: Franki Kohler, Ellen Pahl
Copyeditor: Stacy Chamness
Proofreader: Wordfirm
Cover Designer: Kristen Yenche
Design Director/Book Designer: Kristen Yenche
Illustrator: Richard Sheppard
Production Assistant: Tim Manibusan
Photography: Luke Mulks, Sharon Risedorph, unless otherwise noted
Published by C&T Publishing, Inc., P.O. Box 1456, Lafayette, California, 94549

Front cover: *Serendipity* by M'Liss Rae Hawley

Back cover: *The Big Easy* by M'Liss Rae Hawley

Library of Congress Cataloging-in-Publication Data
Hawley, M'Liss Rae.
 Phenomenal fat quarter quilts : new projects with tips to inspire & enhance your quiltmaking / M'Liss Rae Hawley.
     p. cm.
 Includes index.
 ISBN 1-57120-277-3 (paper trade)
 1. Patchwork--Patterns. 2. Quilting. I. Title.
 TT835.H348523 2004
  746.46'041--dc22
2004008153
Printed in China

10 9 8 7 6 5 4 3 2 1

CONTENTS

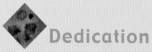

Dedication

For my mother and best friend, Josephine Walsh Frandsen, who—since I was a young girl—understood and appreciated my goals and passions, and supported me every step of the way. Like everyone, I had my ups and downs, and through most of the first 40 years of my life, nearly everyone told me to find another career. But my mother stood by me, confident that one day I would be successful in this industry.

Thank you, Mom!

Acknowledgments

Change is an inevitable part of life. In the past few years I have seen many changes, both personally and professionally. On the personal side, my son joined the Marine Corps and has spent much of the time overseas; my daughter (and assistant) went away to college. My husband was elected to his third and final term as Island County Sheriff and published his second best-selling murder mystery.

Professionally, I have had the opportunity to partner with new people and companies.

I would most gratefully like to thank the following people and their respective companies for sharing my vision, enthusiasm, and love of quilting.

C&T Publishing:
Amy Marson, Publisher

Jan Grigsby, Acquisitions Editor

Darra Williamson, Editorial Consultant

Husqvarna Viking:
Stan Ingraham, Senior V.P., Sales and Marketing

Sue Hausmann, Senior V.P., Education and
    Consumer Motivation

Tony Kowal, Embroidery Design Specialist

Nancy Jewell, Publicity Director

Theresa Robinson, Notions Marketing Specialist

In The Beginning Fabrics:
Sharon Evans Yenter, Owner

Jason Yenter, President

Island Fabrics:
Judy Martin, Owner

Hoffman California Fabrics:
Sandy Muckenthaler, Director of Marketing

Quilters Dream Batting:
Kathy Thompson, Owner

Robison-Anton Textile Company:
Bruce Anton, Owner

Andreea M. Sparhawk, Product Manager

My fat-quarter books are full of many wonderful quilts by very talented people. This book is a testament to their dedication and devotion to quilting. A special thank you to my friend, Susie Kincy and my sister, Erin Rae Frandsen, for their assistance every step of the way.

introduction

We have so many wonderful options when we decide to make a quilt—sometimes I think perhaps *too* many. For beginners especially, the choices can be overwhelming. Quilt stores are full of beautiful fabric, books, and patterns, while shops and guilds offer a dizzying array of classes.

Because of this, one of the first topics I introduce in my lectures and workshops is the need to *reduce your variables.* I encourage quilters simply to pick a theme, decide on a "color story" (or palette), and select a pattern.

Over the years, I have experimented with many strategies to solve the growing sensory overload we quilters face. I want to get people quilting instead of using so much valuable time trying to make decisions. I've discovered that the most effective way to quickly and esthetically *reduce your variables* and still create stunning quilts is to use fat quarters and make fat-quarter quilts.

The patterns I've created follow a simple format: each includes six to eight fat quarters, a background fabric (six in some cases!), and an inner and outer border. Most of the patterns are original, while others represent my fat-quarter interpretation of an old favorite.

If you compare quilting to poetry, fat-quarter quilts relate best to haiku. This ancient Japanese form of verse consists of seventeen syllables distributed over three lines, always in a five, seven, five pattern. Yet, with so few words and a consistent format, the poet can create beautiful verbal and mental images. Likewise, the quilter creates beautiful visual imagery within the limitations imposed by fat-quarter pieces.

Phenomenal Fat Quarter Quilts is my third book on working with fat quarters. I have also created numerous fat-quarter patterns for *McCall's Quilting* and *McCall's Quick Quilts* magazines, as well as two fat-quarter tote bag patterns.

This newest collection includes eight fast and fun patterns. The sizes vary from wallhangings to large lap quilts. This time, I have added a new twist to the fat-quarter family: embellishment. The Embellished Braids pattern (page 42) features rickrack, ribbons, and decorative stitching. If you've never tried it before, this pattern is a great introduction to the world of embellishment.

The Serendipity block (page 46) features three different background fabrics and utilizes a simple partial-seam sewing technique. The finished blocks are placed on point. These characteristics and methods add interest to both the construction process and the result.

I could not do a fat-quarter book without including a machine-embroidered quilt. The Windows pattern (page 54) features a combination of pieced and "framed" embroidered blocks. A secondary pinwheel pattern forms in the corners where the two blocks meet.

The Millennium block (page 50) is a fence rail made with six fat quarters and two background fabrics. The opposing corners of each block feature a quarter circle, which is pieced into the block the "old-fashioned way"—that is, much like a small, set-in sleeve. A two-color circle is formed when four blocks meet.

Likewise, the remaining four patterns introduce other techniques and concepts, each—in the *reduce your variables* tradition—designed to expand your skills with ease and enjoyment.

FAT QUARTER HAIKU
FQ quilts are fun
'Specially when they are done
Start another one

Enjoy!
M'Liss

making
fat–quarter quilts

What You'll Need: Tools

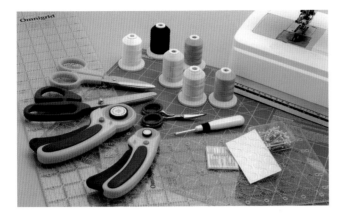

The basic tools and supplies needed to make fat-quarter quilts.

One of the best things about fat-quarter quilts is that you don't need a lot of fancy gadgets or special equipment to make them. The basics, including typical rotary cutting supplies, work perfectly. Here is a list of what you'll need, with thoughts about my personal favorite features.

Rotary cutter: with an ergonomic-style grip and reliable safety catch

Cutting mat: green, with a grid. Lines marking the 45° angle are helpful.

Acrylic rulers: both the 6" x 24" and 6" x 12" sizes, preferably with the 45° angle indicated

Ruler grips: the clear type. These adhesive tabs stick to the bottom of your rulers to keep them from slipping as you cut.

Pins: fine, glass-head silk pins (They don't leave unsightly holes in the fabric.)

Scissors: both fabric scissors and small embroidery-type scissors for cutting thread

Seam ripper: with an ergonomic-style handle

Thread: 100-percent cotton thread in a neutral color for piecing

Sewing machine needles: Keep a good supply on hand to change after each project.

Sewing machine: in good working order, with a ¼" presser foot to help keep piecing accurate. If your machine does not come with this foot, I strongly recommend that you buy one!

Additional attachments: If you plan to machine quilt straight lines and apply binding by machine, a dual-feed or walking foot is a must. For attaching trims, as on Embellished Braids (page 41), a cording or braiding foot makes the job go much more smoothly. Try an open-toe foot for decorative stitching.

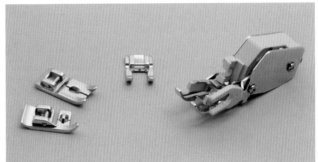

From left to right: narrow braid/cord foot, braiding foot, open-toe foot, and dual-feed foot

Choosing Fabric: The Best Part!

The patterns in the book call for six to eight fat quarters to use as foreground (the primary design or motif), background fabric (can be a single piece or multiple fabrics), and yardage for borders, binding, and backing. We'll start with the fat quarters—naturally!

tip **LAUNDRY DAY!** In my sewing room, the process is a family affair. I prewash all new fabric (fat quarters in the sink, ½ yard and larger pieces in the washing machine). My husband, Michael, does the ironing: straight from the dryer fabrics are ironed, squared up (with the help of our daughter, Adrienne, when she is home from college), and on to the shelf in no time.

What *is* a Fat Quarter?

Unlike a standard quarter yard of fabric, which is cut across the full width of the fabric and measures 9" x 42", a fat quarter is a half yard of fabric (18" x 42") cut in half from top to bottom. Therefore, technically, a fat quarter should measure 18" x 21".

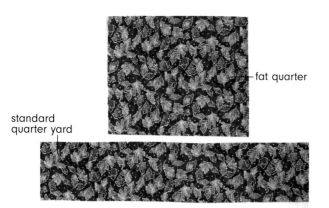

standard
quarter yard

fat quarter

In reality, when you examine different fat-quarter pieces, you may notice slight differences in size, even within the same packet of fabrics. This can happen for a number of reasons. Some manufacturers' fabrics are slightly narrower than the industry standard of 42". Some shops consistently cut their fat quarters slightly larger or smaller. Selvages may eat into the width, affecting the usable dimensions.

What happens after you bring your fabric home can also make a difference in the size of your fat quarters. Prewashing, a practice I advocate, can shrink fabric slightly, and the washing machine has a tendency to fray smaller pieces of fabric.

Because of these variables, I've based the patterns in this book on fat quarters that measure 17½" x 20" after laundering. I suggest that you measure all your fat quarters after you wash them. This can spare you surprise (and frustration) when you begin cutting. Depending on the usable size of your fat quarters, you may want or need to add additional fat quarters.

You may decide to make more or fewer blocks than the instructions call for. As you look at the photos in this book, you'll see quilts of different sizes made from the same pattern. In some cases, the quilters simply—and creatively—made do.

Working with Fat-Quarter Packets

This is the fun part of the process . . . choosing the fabric! Whatever level of quilter you are, prepackaged fat-quarter packets are a great place to start in planning your fat-quarter quilt (see the tip on the top of page 9). Look around! Quilt shops, catalogs, and on-line sources assemble luscious groupings for your convenience—and delight. These handy collections are the ultimate in reducing your variables. Six or eight beautifully coordinating fat quarters make it effortless for the beginner and the more experienced quilter alike.

A wide range of stunning (and convenient!) fat-quarter packets are available at quilt shops, through mail order, or online. See Resources (page 80).

READY, SET, GO! Here are some suggestions for selecting fat-quarter packets, depending upon your skill level. Once you feel comfortable, push yourself to the next level.

Beginners: Go to your favorite quilt shop, catalog, or website, and purchase your favorite packet!

Confident beginners: Do the same, but buy fabric that appears to be a challenge for you!

Intermediate-level quilters: Buy two coordinating packets of six fat quarters, and mix them up!

Totally confident quilters: Get really creative! Mix fat quarters from packets with fat quarters already in your stash, or build your own fat-quarter packets.

Creating Your Own Fat-Quarter Packet

Sometimes you wake up with a wonderful idea for a fat-quarter quilt, only to find that your favorite quilt shop or other fabric resource doesn't have the perfect fat-quarter packet to recreate the "look." Perhaps you want the challenge of building your own fat-quarter packet to make one of the quilts in this book. Where do you begin?

FABRIC LINES! A fabric line is a great way to go about building your own fat-quarter packet and adding border and background fabrics for a quilt. The motifs are designed to harmonize, the colorways are coordinated, and the ultimate look is very together! I used a fabric line I designed when making my quilt *Autumn View on Whidbey Island* (page 78).

I often suggest to my students that they select the quilt pattern first; the pattern may bring a specific fabric or theme to mind. Alternative approaches include the following:

◆ Pick a theme. A holiday, season, or special event can often direct your choice of fabric.

Use holiday, seasonal, and special-event fabrics to jump-start your creativity.

◆ Choose your background or border fabric first. A dark background may dictate different fat-quarter selections than a light background. If you see a potential border fabric that captures your imagination—whether in the quilt shop or already in your stash—this may be the place to start (see pages 12 and 13).

◆ Focus on color. Do you have a favorite color? One that you consider a challenge? A color you've never worked with, but are anxious to try? Use this color as your source of inspiration.

◆ Consider the purpose. Are you wanting a quilt for a specific location in your home? A fat-quarter quilt fills the bill perfectly. Let the decor dictate your fabric choices.

◆ Give—or get—a gift. You may be making the quilt for a lucky friend or relative. Let yourself be guided by their tastes. On the other hand, you may be given the gift of a fat-quarter packet; use that as inspiration for the fat-quarter quilt.

Once you have a starting point, you are ready to choose six to eight fat quarters to make up your own personal packet. As a rule, a variety in prints (pattern and scale), color, and value (lights, mediums, and darks) will make your quilt more interesting.

HOW MUCH TO BUY? When I'm not buying precut or prepackaged fat quarters, I typically purchase a minimum of ⅝ yard off the bolt. This gives me two fat quarters (one to share with a friend, perhaps!) plus a little extra. When I'm choosing fabric for a border, I buy the necessary yardage plus an additional ½ yard in case I wish to include this fabric as a fat quarter, too.

I like to mix it up. I'll choose a plaid, a small-scale blender fabric, a larger-scale print, a subtle tone-on-tone print, and perhaps a print that continues the theme. Stripes are always fun! Don't forget to add a zinger: a fabric that adds a touch of the main color's complement or that picks up an unusual color in the theme fabric. You do not have to love every fabric in your fat-quarter assortment. A mixture of textures, layers of color, and a bold departure from your comfort zone makes for a great fat-quarter quilt.

Aim for a variety of prints (pattern and scale) in your fat-quarter packet.

Value refers to the lightness or darkness of a color in relationship to those around it and is an essential factor in the success of your quilt. Value creates contrast and allows you to see the pattern emerge. Even if you make a one-color quilt (also called monochromatic), the range of light to dark within that single color is what makes the quilt "work."

A variety of red fabrics, ranging from light to dark

Choosing Background Fabric

How important is the background fabric? It is as significant as your choice of fat quarters! Although it may not be the first decision you make, the background fabric may represent up to 50 percent of the pieced quilt. On the other hand, you may have a wonderful piece of background fabric you want to build your quilt around.

The background requirements for the patterns in this book vary from a single piece of yardage (e.g., Portuguese Tiles on page 35) to six different fat quarters (e.g., Pinwheels on page 28). Personally, I love the look of multiple backgrounds. The variety adds depth, texture, and visual interest.

Let the style, proportion, and dimension of the block or pattern guide you in determining the number of background fabrics. For example, the aforementioned Pinwheels pattern is created by the repetition of a single, simple shape: the right-angle triangle. While the addition of multiple background fabrics doesn't add a bit to the difficulty of constructing the quilt, the diversity goes a long way in adding to the quilt's visual appeal. The design already features a half dozen different foreground (pinwheel) fabrics; why not "mix up" the backgrounds as well? Rather than a single background fabric, why not six? Instead of six, why not a dozen? The contrast in visual textures (prints) and the slight variations in value (lights and darks) all add to the richness of the design.

On the other hand, London Roads (page 38) is composed of lots of pieces and many units. The introduction of multiple background fabrics makes less sense here; in fact, the use of multiple background fabrics might prove downright distracting.

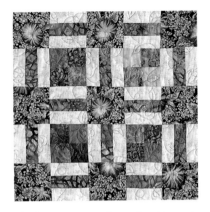

London Roads features a variety of units and variously sized strips and squares to achieve its dynamic overall design. The addition of multiple background fabrics could easily overwhelm the eye.

Background fabrics are often lighter in value, to create a nice contrast with foreground fat-quarter fabrics. Of course, this is not an absolute! Assess *your* fat-quarter assortment. Depending on what you see, you may prefer to go darker for your background. The result isn't "wrong"—just different.

Quilters often choose neutral colors for backgrounds. Technically, neutral means "free from color" (e.g., white, gray, and black), but I like to think that quilters may take liberty and add their own personal neutral colors to the standard list. Your neutral may simply be your favorite color in its lightest value.

The Pinwheel pattern, with its single, repeating triangle shape, gets a visual boost with a variety of both foreground and background fabrics.

I have three colors that I personally consider my quilter's neutrals: yellow, green, and pink. When I find fabrics in a light version of any of these colors, they go straight to the cutting counter. Fabric colors are seasonal and regional; buy what you like when you see it!

Traditional neutrals…and M'Liss's neutrals

 THREAD COLOR! Expanding your scope of neutrals is a great way to look at thread as well. Buy several spools of your personal "quilter's neutrals" when they go on sale. Use these for all your machine piecing.

As always, you can take your cue from the theme fabric. Is the lightest value white or beige? Does the fabric lend itself to a colored background—your personal quilter's neutral? Finding the right background fabric(s) for your fat-quarter quilt is just another step in a wonderful journey. Take time in making choices now. The end results will be well worth it.

Choosing Border Fabrics

Some of the patterns in this book, such as Quilt Interrupted (page 32), are framed with a single outer border. Others, such as Millennium (page 50), include a narrow inner border between the center quilt design and the outer frame. Either way, you'll want to choose border fabrics that complement and enhance your design, rather than overpower it.

Many prepackaged fat-quarter packets are cut from fabrics that have just arrived at your local quilt shop. As a result, the fabrics in the packet are usually still available on the bolt. Repeating one of the fat quarters as your border fabric is a "can't miss" method for finishing your quilt.

 FABRIC FLOAT! Cut the inner border strips from the same fabric as the block background fabric, and the inner design will appear to float within the outer border. See *Purple Dreams* (page 64), Barbara Higbee-Price's interpretation of Portuguese Tiles, for an example of this optical illusion.

SHORT ON BORDER FABRIC? Corner stones—pieced, plain, or embellished—are a great way to extend your border fabric and add design power, too. See my quilt *The Big Easy* (page 28) for confirmation... and inspiration!

Large-scale prints make great outer borders for fat-quarter quilts—as you can see from many of the quilts in this book! You'll need to plan ahead though. Some large-scale prints are pictorial or directional, so they may require extra yardage, as well as extra time and effort in the planning and cutting.

Examples of large-scale directional border fabrics

PARIS FASHION! Take the time to make sure those models do not go the way of Marie Antoinette!

Susie Kincy was careful in cutting her border fabric to make sure that no one lost her head. For a full view of her quilt *Paris Fashion*, see page 73.

There are many other options for selecting an appropriate border fabric:

◆ Misunderstood, overlooked, and often under used, striped fabrics make fabulous borders. Check out *Iznik* (page 65) and *Blowing in the Wind* (page 59), and see for yourself!

◆ If your quilt features a wide range of prints or colors, a multicolored paisley or floral can tie them together. *Happiness* (page 60) is a good example.

◆ *Aged to Perfection* (page 63) demonstrates the success of a border fabric chosen to reflect the quilt's theme.

◆ Try going just a shade darker than the darkest fat-quarter fabric, as in *Sweet and Fun with a Little Bit of Fancy* (page 72).

No doubt you'll come up with many of your own creative solutions.

BLACK OR GOLD! When you are choosing a fabric for an inner border, try several different black and/or gold fabrics. You may discover the perfect transition between the center of the quilt and the outer border.

Choosing Binding Fabric

The binding is usually either the darkest fabric in the quilt or one that repeats the fabric in the outer border. I like to continue the motif or theme of the outer border in my choice of binding fabric. If, for instance, I use a floral print in the outer border, I'll use the same or another, similar floral print as binding.

Rotary Cutting: From Fabrics to Strips

The process for rotary cutting fat quarters is pretty much the same as for cutting yardages, except the pieces are smaller! The following guidelines work for both.

Squaring Your Fabric

It is essential that you square the edges of all your fabrics before you rotary cut them into strips. This is especially important with fat quarters. The piece of fabric is small, and every inch is precious.

The edge must be straight for the strips to be straight, and you don't want to waste a bit by having to recut.

Often students ask me why they have had problems with bows, curves, or "kinks" in their rotary-cut strips. Usually the answer is that the fabric has been folded off grain. You can avoid this by making sure the fabric is pressed and that you fold it *carefully* before you begin to cut. Here's the method I use for folding:

1. Fold the fabric from selvage to selvage (full-width fabric) or selvage to cut edge (fat quarter).

2. Hold the fabric in the air and study the drape. Disregard the cut ends; instead, move the selvages from side to side until the fabric is perfectly flat.

3. Stop, set the fabric on your cutting surface, and make the second fold: selvage edge to folded edge. If you have a large piece of yardage, try to break it down so you can work with a more manageable amount.

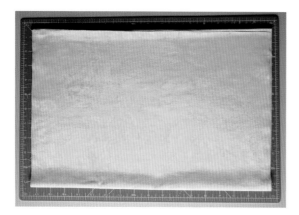

If you are squaring up a fat quarter, you just need to make the first fold from selvage to cut edge. If there is no selvage to guide you, make the fold lengthwise grain to lengthwise grain. You can easily tell the lengthwise grain: it's the edge of the fabric that has no stretch.

To square up your fabric:

1. Place the folded fabric on the cutting mat, with the fold facing you. Position your ruler on the right-hand edge of the fabric, so it is perpendicular to the fold.

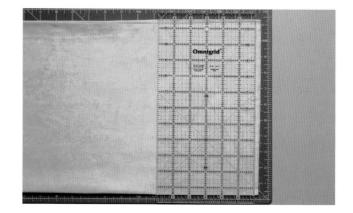

2. Trim a narrow strip from the edge of the fabric to square it up.

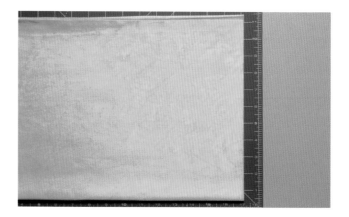

3. Rotate the fabric (or the mat), and repeat to trim the opposite edge.

Cutting Strips

For all quilts in this book you will cut strips from the 20" edge of the fat-quarter piece. Whether you are cutting fat quarters or yardages, use your ruler to measure and cut the strips, not the mat. I use the mat grid to align the fabric and for taking general measurements.

Working from the squared left edge of the fabric, use your ruler to measure and cut a strip of the desired width. Repeat to cut the required number of strips. You may want to square up the end of the fabric after every few cuts.

1. Working from the squared right edge of the fabric, use a ruler to measure the width of the strip you wish to cut. If you are left-handed, cut the strip.

2. If you are right-handed, place a second ruler against the left edge of the first ruler.

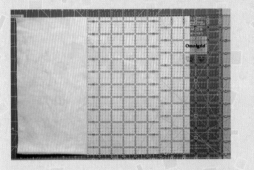

3. Remove the first ruler and cut along the right edge of the ruler that remains.

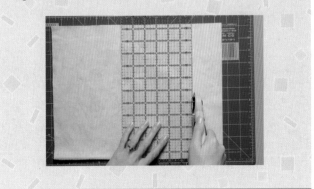

Putting It Together: Basic How-Tos

Once the fabric is chosen, prepared, and cut, it's time to begin assembling the pieces into a quilt!

Piecing and Pressing

Unless noted otherwise, you'll be using a ¼"-wide seam allowance for piecing the quilts in this book. It's always a good idea to check that your ¼" seam is accurate before beginning to sew.

For most projects, you'll sew pieces into units, units into rows, and rows together to complete the blocks. Project instructions will tell you which way to press the seams, either in the step itself or with arrows in the accompanying diagrams.

Press lightly in a lifting-and-lowering motion. Dragging the iron across the fabric can distort the individual pieces and finished blocks.

Assembling the Quilt

Most of the quilts in this book are sewn together in a basic arrangement called the straight set. In this set, the blocks are arranged in horizontal rows, with the block edges parallel to the sides of the quilt. The blocks are sewn together with ¼"-wide seams to create the rows, with seams pressed in opposite directions from row to row. Then the rows are sewn together, and seams pressed, usually in one direction.

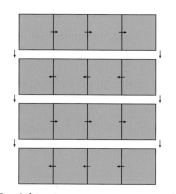

Straight set
Arrows indicate pressing direction.

The blocks in *Serendipity* (page 46) are arranged in a traditional diagonal or on-point set. In this set, the blocks are arranged in diagonal rows, with the block edges at a 45° angle to the sides of the quilt. The zigzag edges are filled in with half- and quarter-square triangles to "straighten" the quilt top. (The project instructions tell you how many of these triangles to cut and how big to cut them.) The blocks and side triangles are sewn together with ¼"-wide seams to create the diagonal rows, with seams pressed in opposite directions from row to row. The corner triangles are added next, and finally the rows are sewn together and pressed.

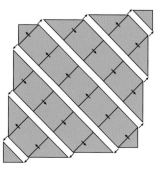

Diagonal set
Arrows indicate pressing direction.

Embellished Braids (page 41) is an example of the traditional coins configuration. The quilt is assembled in rows—usually vertical rows—instead of blocks, and then the rows are sewn together, often with strips of sashing in between and with seams pressed toward the sashing strips.

Adding Borders

The quilts in this book include three different border treatments: squared borders, borders with corner squares, and mitered borders. Here are the instructions to do all three.

BORDER FABRIC! When you complete the top and are getting ready to add the borders, you may find that your original choice of border fabric no longer works. Nevertheless, it served its purpose: it brought you to this point . . . and you now have the start of another project!

Squared Borders

These are the easiest of all borders. Add the top and bottom borders first and then the sides.

1. Measure the finished quilt top through the center from side to side. Cut two borders to this measurement; these will be the top and bottom borders.

2. Place pins at the center point of the top and bottom of the quilt top, as well as at the center point of each border strip. Pin the borders to the quilt top, matching the ends and center points. Use additional pins as needed, easing or gently stretching the border to fit.

3. Sew the borders to the quilt top with a ¼"-wide seam. Press as instructed—usually toward the border. If the quilt top is slightly longer than the border, stitch with the quilt top on the bottom, closest to the feed dogs. If the reverse is true, stitch with the border on the bottom. The motion of the feed dogs will help ease in the extra length.

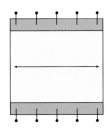

4. Measure the quilt from top to bottom, including the borders you've just sewn. Cut two borders to this measurement; these will be the side borders. Repeat Steps 2 and 3 to pin, sew, and press the borders.

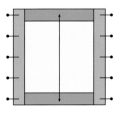

Borders with Corner Squares

Instructions for the Pinwheels pattern (page 28) include borders with corner squares. You'll notice that some of the other quilts include this option as well.

1. Measure the quilt top through the center from side to side and from top to bottom. Cut two border strips to each of these measurements.

2. Sew the appropriately sized strips to the top and bottom of the quilt. Press the seams toward the border. Sew the corner square to each end of the remaining border strips. Press the seams toward the border strip. Sew to the sides of the quilt; press.

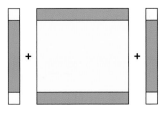

SIZING SOLUTION! It's easy to figure the size you need to cut the corner square: the unfinished size of the corner square = the unfinished width of the border. So, for example, a border cut 4½" wide needs a 4½" (unfinished) corner square.

Machine Embroidery TIPS

I love machine embroidery and often incorporate it into my quilt designs. The Windows pattern (page 54) includes blocks that feature machine embroidery. Other patterns, such as Pinwheels (page 28), suggest optional machine-embroidered corner squares. These are just a few ideas for introducing the beauty of machine embroidery to your quilts. I'm sure you'll think of many others.

Here are some tips to help you get started:

◆ Prewash the fabric you plan to use as background for the embroidery designs. Washing will also preshrink the fabric . . . a necessary step!

◆ Begin with a fresh, new needle, and change it during the process if the point becomes dull. Skipped stitches are one indication of a dull needle. Some embroidery designs have an excess of 10,000 stitches. A dull needle can distort the design.

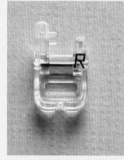

◆ Outfit your machine with an embroidery-foot attachment.

◆ Prewind several bobbins with polyester or cotton bobbin-fill thread, such as Robison-Anton polyfilament bobbin thread. As an alternative, you can purchase pre-wound bobbins, such as those manufactured by Robison-Anton. Choose white or black, using the background fabric as your guide. You may want to change the bobbin thread as the color of the top thread changes.

◆ Select a fabric stabilizer to use under the background fabric. There are many different types of stabilizers available; whichever you choose, read the manufacturer's instructions *carefully*. Some stabilizers are heat- or water-sensitive. I prefer a tear-away stabilizer when I machine embroider on 100% cotton fabric. Sometimes a liquid stabilizer works well with a lightweight or light-colored fabric. If the fabric is prone to puckering, try a water- or heat-soluble stabilizer.

Stabilizers

◆ A hoop is key; it keeps the fabric from shifting as you embroider the designs. If possible, place the fabric in the hoop so it is on the straight grain. Avoid puckers and pleats. The fabric should be taut, but not pulled too tightly.

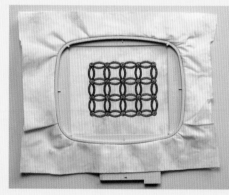

◆ Stitch a test of the desired embroidery design, using the fabric, threads, and stabilizer you plan to use for the project. You'll be able to tell if the thread tension is correct, if the thread coverage is sufficient, and how the embroidered design will look on the background fabric, so you can make any necessary adjustments. If you wish, you can incorporate your test design into your label or quilt backing.

Mitered Borders

1. Measure the finished quilt top through the center from top to bottom to find the length of the quilt. Add two times the width of the border, plus 5" for insurance. Cut two borders to this measurement; these will be the *side* borders. Measure the finished quilt top from side to side to find the width of the quilt. Add two times the width of the border, plus 5"; these will be the *top and bottom* borders.

2. Place pins to mark the center of all sides of the quilt top, as well as the center point of each border strip.

3. Measure and pin-mark *half the length* of the quilt top on both sides of the center pin on each side border strip. Pin the borders to the sides of the quilt, matching center point to center point, and match the pins marking the quilt length on the border strip to the edges of the quilt top. (The excess border length will extend beyond each edge of the quilt.)

4. Stitch the border strips to the sides of the quilt, stopping ¼" from the edge of the quilt with a backstitch. Press seams toward the borders.

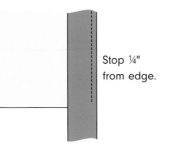

Stop ¼"
from edge.

5. Repeat Steps 3 and 4 to pin and sew the top and bottom borders to the quilt; press. The border strips extend beyond each end.

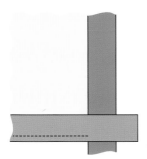

6. To create the miter, lay one corner of the quilt right side up on your ironing board. Working with the quilt right side up, place the excess "tail" of one border strip on top of the adjacent border. Fold the top border strip under at a 45° angle so it meets the edge of the bottom border. Lightly press the fold in place.

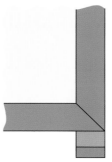

7. Use a ruler or right-angle triangle to be certain the angle is correct and the corner is square, and press again, firmly.

8. Fold the quilt top diagonally, right sides together, and align the 45° fold marks and the long edges of the border strips. Place pins near the pressed fold to secure the corners of the border strips for sewing.

9. Beginning with a backstitch at the inside corner of the border, carefully stitch toward the outside edge along the fold. Finish with a backstitch.

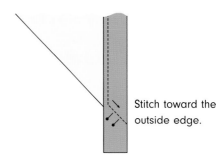

Stitch toward the outside edge.

10. Trim the excess border fabric to ¼"-wide seam allowance and press the seam open.

Finishing Your Quilt: Final Touches

Quilting, bindings, hanging sleeve, label . . . these final touches are important, so be sure to give them the same attention you've given to every other step of the process.

Preparing Your Quilt for Quilting

As with every step of quiltmaking, this step is important. Don't skimp here. Take time to layer properly and baste sufficiently. The results—a nice flat quilt, free from puckers and bumps—will make you proud!

Batting

Choice of batting is a personal decision, but you'll want to consider the method (and amount) of quilting, and the quilt's end use. Since I prefer machine quilting I usually use cotton batting in a heavier weight for bed quilts and wallhangings and a lighter weight for clothing. You'll probably want to stick with lightweight batting for hand quilting. Polyester batting is a good choice for tied quilts.

Cut the batting approximately 4" larger than the quilt top on all sides.

Backing

As with the batting, you'll want the quilt backing to be approximately 4" larger than the quilt top on all sides. You'll sometimes need to piece the fabric to have a large enough piece. Prewash the backing fabric, and remove the selvages first.

Layering and Basting

Unlike many machine quilters, I prefer to hand baste with thread rather than to pin baste. This allows me to machine quilt without stopping to remove pins.

1. Carefully press the quilt top from the back to set the seams, and then press from the front. Press the backing. If you wish, use spray starch or sizing.

2. Spread the backing wrong side up on a clean, flat surface and secure it with masking tape. The fabric should be taut but not stretched. Center the batting, and then the quilt top right side up over the backing and secure.

3. Thread a long needle with light-colored thread. Beginning in the center, hand baste a 4" grid of horizontal and vertical lines.

4. After basting the quilt, remove the tape and get ready to quilt!

Quilting

Whether you choose to hand quilt, machine quilt, or even combine the two techniques, you'll find the patterns in this book are loaded with quilting possibilities. Experiment with different techniques, threads, and thread colors. Don't overlook the potential for embellishments, such as couching, bobbin work, or other decorative stitching to add "quilting" as you go.

Sources for quilting designs are everywhere. While quilting in-the-ditch or outline quilting (stitching ¼" inside each shape) are always options, don't forget to explore the many choices available in quilting stencils and books of quilting patterns. Examine your fabrics; perhaps there is a motif or pattern you can adapt for free-motion quilting. Or do as I often do, and design machine-quilting patterns as you quilt. Begin with a vague overall plan, and allow yourself creative freedom as you move around the top. Remember: you are the best judge of which quilting designs best complement your work!

Squaring Up

Before adding the binding, you need to trim the excess batting and backing and square up your quilt. Use the seam of the outer border as a guide.

1. Align a ruler with the outer border seam and measure to the edge of the quilt in a number of places. Use the narrowest measurement as a guide for positioning your ruler, and trim the excess batting and backing all around the quilt.

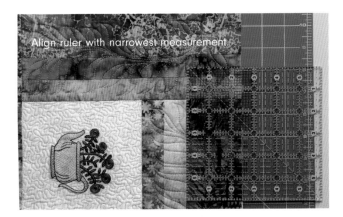

2. Fold the quilt in half lengthwise and crosswise to check that the corners are square and the sides are equal in length. If not, use a square ruler to correct this one corner at a time.

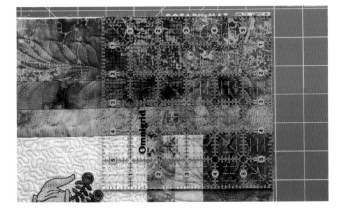

3. Stabilize the edges of the quilt by stitching around the perimeter with a basting or serpentine stitch. (Do not use a zigzag stitch.)

Serpentine stitch

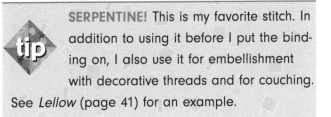

SERPENTINE! This is my favorite stitch. In addition to using it before I put the binding on, I also use it for embellishment with decorative threads and for couching. See *Lellow* (page 41) for an example.

4. Remove any stray threads or bits of batting from the quilt top, and you are ready to bind your quilt.

Making and Applying Binding

Binding is an important and, sadly, often overlooked step in the quiltmaking process. Many a wonderful quilt is spoiled by a poorly sewn binding. Take time in deciding what fabric you will use, and enjoy the process of stitching it to your quilt. You're coming down the home stretch now!

The following method is the one I use to bind my quilts. It results in a finished edge that is attractive and strong.

I typically cut binding strips 3"- wide from selvage to selvage across the width of the fabric. I make an exception and cut strips on the bias only to create a special effect with a plaid or striped fabric or when I need to follow a curved or rounded edge.

BINDING EXTRAVAGANZA! Keep the fat-quarter fun going. Cut 3"- wide strips from a variety of your fat-quarter fabrics and piece them to make the binding. See *Technicolor Hugs and Kisses* (page 64) for a brilliant example.

1. Cut enough binding strips to go around the perimeter (outside edges) of the quilt, plus an extra 10" for seams and corners. Sew the strips together at right angles, as shown. Trim the excess fabric, leaving a ¼"-wide seam allowance, and press the seams open.

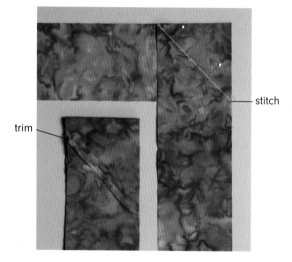

trim

stitch

2. Fold the binding in half lengthwise, wrong sides together, and press.

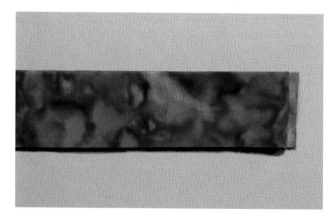

3. Starting 6" from the upper left-hand corner, and with the raw edges even, lay the binding on the quilt top. Check to see that none of the mitered seams falls on a corner of the quilt. If it does, adjust the starting point. Begin stitching 4" from the end of the binding, using a ½"-wide seam allowance.

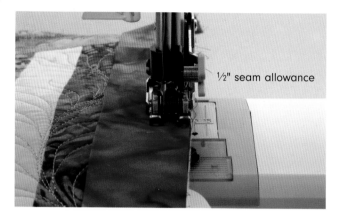

½" seam allowance

4. Stitch about 2", stop, and cut the threads. Remove the quilt from under the machine and fold the binding to the back of the quilt. The binding should cover the line of machine stitching. If the binding overlaps the stitching too much, try again, stitching just outside the first line of stitching. If the binding doesn't cover the original line of stitching, stitch just inside the line. Remove the unwanted stitches before you continue.

5. Using the position you determined for stitching in Step 4, continue stitching to within ½" of the first corner of the quilt. Stop, cut the thread, and remove the quilt from the machine.

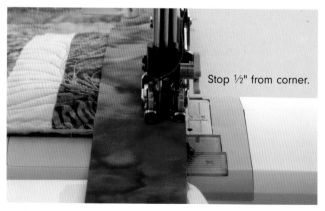

Stop ½" from corner.

6. Fold the binding as shown to create a mitered corner.

Fold binding up.

7. Bring binding strip down, even with the edge of the quilt. Resume stitching, ½" from the edge, mitering each corner as you come to it.

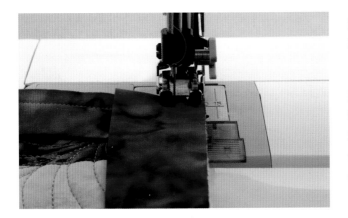

8. Stop stitching about 3" after you've turned the last corner. Make sure the starting and finishing ends of the binding overlap by at least 4". Cut the threads and remove the quilt from the machine. Measure a 3" overlap and trim the excess binding.

9. Lay the quilt right side up. Unfold the unstitched tails, place them right sides together at right angles, and pin. Draw a line from the upper left corner to the lower right corner of the binding as shown and stitch on the drawn line.

10. Carefully trim the seam allowances to ¼" and press the seam open. Refold the binding and press. Finish stitching the binding to the quilt.

11. Turn the binding to the back of the quilt and pin. (I pin approximately 12" at a time.) Use matching-colored thread to stitch the binding to the quilt back, carefully mitering the corners as you approach them. Hand stitch the miters on both the front and the back of the quilt.

Making and Adding a Sleeve

If you want to display your quilt on a wall, you need a sleeve to protect your work of art from undue strain.

1. Cut an 8½"-wide strip of backing fabric 1" shorter than the width of the quilt. (If the quilt is wider than 40", cut 2 strips and stitch them together, end to end.) Fold the short ends under ¼", stitch, and press.

2. Fold the sleeve lengthwise, right sides together. Sew the long raw edges and press. Turn the sleeve right side out, and press again.

3. Match the center point of the top edge of the quilt with the center point of the sleeve. Pin the sleeve to the quilt, right below the binding. Use matching-colored thread to blindstitch the top edge of the sleeve in place.

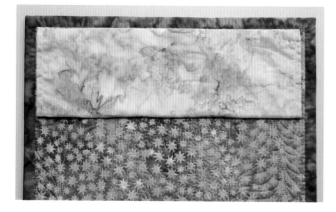

4. Push the bottom edge of the sleeve up a tiny bit so that when inserted, the hanging rod does not put strain on the quilt. Blindstitch the bottom edge of the sleeve, taking care not to catch the front of the quilt as you stitch.

Creating a Label

I always recommend that you make a label for your quilt. This gives you a place to provide important information about both you and the quilt. I like to make my labels large—about 4" x 7"—so I have plenty of room. You can sew the label to the lower right corner of the quilt back before it is quilted, or wait until after the quilt is finished.

I suggest you include the following information on your label: the name of the quilt; your full name (and business name, if you have one); your city, county, province and/or state, and country of residence; and the date.

If the quilt was made for a special person, to commemorate a special event, or as part of a series, you may want to include this information as well. You may also choose to note the name of the quilting teacher who inspired you or tell a special story connected to the quilt.

You can make a simple label by drawing and writing on fabric with permanent fabric markers. (Stabilize the fabric first with freezer paper or interfacing.) For a more elaborate (and fun!) label, try photo-transfer techniques, use the lettering system on your sewing machine, or use an embroidery machine to embellish your label. You may even want to create your own distinctive signature or logo. Include patches, decals, buttons, ribbons, or lace. I often include leftover blocks to tie the quilt top to the back.

This is the label on my Spring View Through Rose-Colored Glasses *quilt (page 54).*

Designing Your Own Fat-Quarter Quilts

In pages 7-13 I've suggested various approaches to selecting the fabrics for your fat-quarter quilt. I've included methods of working with prepackaged groupings of six to eight fat quarters, and how to assemble a grouping of your own from the fabrics already in your stash or on the shelves of your local quilt shop. I've discussed the process of evaluating fabrics to find the ideal backgrounds, borders, and bindings to complement your fat-quarter selections.

Once you've made these fabric decisions, you are ready to tackle any and all of the projects in this book. Suppose, however, that you'd like to try your hand at designing your own fat-quarter-friendly quilt? Where do you begin? Are there any specific size or design factors you should consider?

Design Considerations

Fat-quarter quilts are all about reducing your variables. The first and foremost consideration in designing a fat-quarter quilt is the limitation imposed by the size of the individual pieces of fabric (approximately 18" x 20"). Rather than seeing this as a restriction or lia-bility, I actually find it to be very liberating. Consider it this way: these are the ingredients you have to bake your cake. The number and quantity is finite. Sure it's a challenge . . . but don't you love a challenge?

QUILT SIZE? No limits! Working with fat quarters doesn't mean you can only make small-scale quilts. The size of the fat quarter dictates the size of the blocks or units, not the overall size of the quilt. Full-size, queen-size, even king-size: the sky's the limit!

I generally work in two ways when I design a fat-quarter quilt. I begin either with a traditional block (as I did for Pinwheels on page 28) or design my own (as I did for Portuguese Tiles on page 35).

Starting with a Traditional Block

When I choose a traditional block as the starting point for my design, I must first decide what size the block should be to optimize the dimensions of the fat-quarter. To do this, I usually rely on graph paper and my calculator.

As I am somewhat "computer challenged," I begin by drawing the block full-size on 10-to-the-inch graph paper. Once I've drawn the pattern on paper, I can determine how many shapes are involved, how many of each shape I need, and what size the shapes need to be. This gives me all the basic information I need to determine whether or not I can cut the necessary shapes from a piece of fabric approximately 18" x 20". It also gives me a visual reference for exploring options for quick-cutting and piecing methods such as strip-piecing or half-square triangle techniques.

Sometimes the process takes a little "tweaking," but again, I consider this a wonderful, creative adventure. What if I were to slightly reduce (or enlarge) the size of the block? Can I (or do I want to) repeat the same combination of fabrics in more than one block? Would the pattern support (or even benefit from) a more scrappy look? Suppose I were to add (or elimi-nate) a fat quarter? Would an alternative method of cutting or piecing make a difference?

ON POINT! Rotate the blocks. The result looks different: more sophisticated and more interesting. On-point sets also *look* harder to do (although they are not!), giving your quilt "viewer points" for a higher degree of difficulty. This is good!

Starting from Scratch

When I create a design from scratch, I follow basically the same steps as I do for a traditional pattern, although I usually test the success of my idea before moving on. Once I've got the idea on paper, I actually make a sample block in scrap fabric. Sometimes I hit it absolutely right the first time. Other times a little adjustment does the trick. Very often, I find the solution is to simplify the design a bit; for example, eliminate a seam or a shape. Sometimes I just need to make the block a bit smaller to get the necessary yield from my fat-quarter pieces. Recreating the block in fabric helps me visualize the possibilities.

Sometimes the idea just needs a little time to percolate. I have resealable bags full of these design attempts. I don't consider them "unsuccessful," and I never throw a design away. Some of my previously rejected ideas find new life in another form. The Quilt Interrupted pattern (page 32) is a perfect example. I was never completely satisfied with my original design; something about it just didn't seem right, and all of my attempts to fix it met with disappointment. Into a resealable bag it went! As I started to play with design ideas for this book, I pulled out my collection of "not-quite" patterns. Quilt Interrupted

seemed to beckon. I knew I wanted the effect of a lattice over a simple block of two subtly contrasting backgrounds. I began to play with the scale of the pieces, particularly the width of the lattice strips, and discovered that—in this case—smaller was definitely the solution. With just a bit of tinkering, I had discovered a wonderful new look.

The moral of the story? Sometimes an idea does not work out as originally planned, but given a bit of time and patience, it evolves into something entirely different—and often better. This happens to me often enough that I've learned to trust my instincts and not give up too quickly. Some of my best designs happen this way!

Give it a try. Creating your own fat-quarter designs is so much fun!

OUTSIDE THE BOX! Don't be afraid to look beyond the boundaries of a square block. You can stretch your block into a rectangle, as I did with Portuguese Tiles (page 35). You can even eliminate the confines of the block completely: build the entire quilt top from simple shapes and units.

Projects
& Patterns

Pinwheels

The Big Easy, designed and made by M'Liss Rae Hawley, machine quilted by Barbara Dau, 2003.

T he Pinwheel block is a classic quilt pattern, made from four half-square triangle units. This version features six fat-quarter foreground fabrics (for the pinwheels themselves), and six fat-quarter background fabrics, making for a wonderfully scrappy-looking quilt.

For fun, I added embroidery and appliqué to the corner squares of The Big Easy (page 28). The pattern also has optional pieced corner squares.

Pinwheels is the easiest pattern in the book, and the quilt top goes together very quickly. You may want to make more than one, each in a different color combination.

 ONE-COLOR WONDER! Select a simple **tip** pattern (Pinwheel is perfect!), a favorite color, mix it with a neutral such as white, and you are good to go! See *Double Dutch* (page 61) and you'll agree.

Materials

All yardage is based on 40"-wide fabric, unless otherwise noted.

6 fat quarters (3 medium and 3 dark value) for block foregrounds

6 fat quarters (light value) for block backgrounds*

½ yard for inner border and outer border corner squares

1 yard for outer border

4 yards for backing

⅝ yard for binding

½ yard for hanging sleeve

59" x 72" piece of batting

May substitute 1½ yards of a single fabric.

Cutting

Cut along the 20" length of the fat quarters. Refer to What *is* a Fat Quarter? (page 8).

From *each* fat-quarter foreground:

Cut 4 strips, 4¼" x 20".

From *each* fat-quarter background:

Cut 4 strips, 4¼" x 20".

From the ½ yard of fabric:

Cut 5 strips, 1½" x 40".

Cut 4 squares, 5½" x 5½".*

From the outer border fabric:

Cut 5 strips, 5½" x 40".

From the binding fabric:

Cut 6 strips, 3" x 40".

From the hanging sleeve fabric:

Cut 2 strips, 8½" x 40".

* *See the tip on page 31 for corner square options.*

 6 + 6 = 12! Six foreground plus six **tip** background fat quarters—the more the merrier! Mix and match them for another original fat-quarter look—this time, totally scrappy.

Pinwheel Blocks

1. Layer each 4¼" x 20" foreground strip with a 4¼" x 20" background strip, right sides together, randomly mixing the combinations. Crosscut each pairing into 4 squares, 4¼" x 4¼" (96 pairs total). Cut each layered square once diagonally.

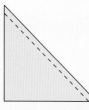

Cut 96 layered squares once diagonally.

2. Sew each triangle pair together along the bias edge. Press the seam toward the dark fabric. Square up the unit to 3¾". Make 192 half-square triangle units.

Make 192.

3. Lay out 4 half-square triangle units as shown. Match the foreground fabrics, but mix the background fabrics within the block. Sew the block together; press. Make 48 blocks.

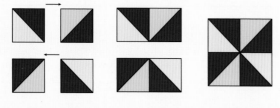

Make 48.

Assembling the Quilt Top

1. Arrange the blocks in 8 horizontal rows of 6 blocks each, as shown in the quilt diagram below. Sew the blocks into rows. Press the seams in alternating directions from row to row. Sew the rows together; press.

Quilt diagram

> **SIMPLE SCRAMBLE!** Here's an easy way to scatter your Pinwheel blocks. Label the blocks 1–6 based on the foreground fabric. Lay out the first row: 1–6; the second row: 2–6, and 1; the third row: 3–6, 1, and 2; and so on for all 8 rows.

2. Refer to Squared Borders (page 17). Measure, trim, and sew an inner border strip to the top and bottom of the quilt. Press the seams toward the border. Repeat to sew inner borders to the sides, piecing as necessary.

3. Refer to Borders with Corner Squares (page 17). Measure the quilt through the center from side to side and from top to bottom. Trim 2 outer border strips to each of these measurements, piecing as necessary.

4. Sew the shorter outer border strips to the top and bottom of the quilt. Press the seams toward the outer border. Sew a 5½" x 5½" square to each end of the longer outer border strips. Press the seams toward the border strip. Sew to the sides of the quilt; press.

OPTIONS GALORE! You can keep the corner squares simple, as described above, for a terrific-looking quilt. However, if you have an embroidery collection or ideas for appliqué that carry on your theme, be creative and go for it, as I did in the corner squares of *The Big Easy.* (See Machine Embroidery Tips on page 18 and Resources on page 80.)
Just remember to allow extra fabric to fit in your embroidery hoop, and trim to size afterward. For yet another alternative, pieced-pinwheel corner squares look great and echo the pattern and theme of the quilt. Instructions follow.

Optional Pinwheel Corner Squares

You will need 1 fat quarter *each* for foreground and background. Cut 8 squares 3½" x 3½" from each fabric.

1. Pair each 3½" foreground square with a 3½" background square, right sides together, and cut once diagonally. Sew each triangle pair together along the bias edge. Press the seam toward the dark fabric. Make 16 half-square triangle units. Square up the units to 3" x 3".

2. Arrange and sew 4 half-square triangle units together as described in Pinwheel Blocks, Step 3 (page 30). Your blocks should measure 5½" square. Make 4 blocks.

3. Refer to Assembling the Quilt Top, Steps 3 and 4 on this page, to sew the borders to the quilt , substituting the pieced pinwheels for the 5½" squares.

Detail of pieced corners on my quilt Blowing in the Wind. *For a full view of this quilt, see page 59.*

Finishing

Refer to Finishing Your Quilt (page 20).

1. Piece the backing as described on page 20.

2. Layer the quilt top, batting, and backing; baste.

3. Hand or machine quilt as desired.

4. Use the 3"-wide strips to bind the edges of the quilt.

5. Add a hanging sleeve and label if desired.

Quilt Interrupted

Quilt: *Asian Outlook*

Finished quilt: 38" x 46"

Finished block: 4"

Asian Outlook, designed and made by M'Liss Rae Hawley, machine quilted by Barbara Dau, 2003.

*H*ow many times are you interrupted while you are quilting? Well, this is the quilt for you! This pattern is a great showcase for theme fabrics. Select eight fabrics fairly close in value, and two similar light or dark backgrounds, and you are on your way. The "interruption"—or lattice—is actually the background.

You are going to love this quilt! The pattern comes together so easily, you will want to make a quilt for every occasion.

Materials

All yardage is based on 40"-wide fabric, unless otherwise stated.

8 fat quarters of similar value and consistent theme for block triangles and binding

1/3 yard *each* of 2 same-colored, similar fabrics for lattice strips*

5/8 yard for outer border

3 yards for backing

1/4 yard for hanging sleeve

46" x 54" piece of batting

* *These fabrics should be substantially lighter or darker than the 8 fat quarters.*

Cutting

Cut along the 20" length of the fat quarters. Refer to What *is* a Fat Quarter? (page 8).

From *each* of 4 fat quarters:
Cut 1 strip, 3" x 20".

Cut 3 strips, 4¾" x 20"; crosscut each into 4 squares, 4¾" x 4¾". Cut each square once diagonally to yield 24 half-square triangles (96 half-square triangles total).

From *each* of 4 remaining fat quarters:
Cut 2 strips, 3" x 20".

Cut 2 strips, 4¾" x 20"; crosscut each into 4 squares, 4¾" x 4¾". Cut each square once diagonally to yield 16 half-square triangles (64 half-square triangles total).

From *each* lattice fabric:
Cut 8 strips, 1" x 40"; crosscut into 40 strips, 1" x 6¾" (80 strips total). Label one fabric A and the other B.

From the border fabric:
Cut 5 strips, 3½" x 40".

From the hanging sleeve fabric:
Cut 1 strip, 8½" x 40".

Quilt Interrupted Blocks

1. Divide the half-square triangles from each fat quarter into two equal stacks. Combine one stack of each fabric to make two large stacks of 80 triangles each. Put 1" x 6¾" A strips with one stack, and label it stack A. Put 1" x 6¾" B strips with the other stack, and label it stack B.

2. Select two different half-square triangles and a 1" x 6¾" strip from stack A. With right sides together and raw edges aligned, place the A strip along the long (bias) edge of one triangle. Match the long edges, point to point. With the strip on top, sew the triangle and strip together with a ¼" seam. Press the seam *toward* the triangle. Make 40.

Make 40.

3. With right sides together and the strip on top, sew the remaining triangle to the opposite edge of the strip. Press the seam toward the triangle. Make 40, and label them Block A.

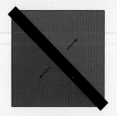

Make 40 of Block A.

4. Repeat Steps 2 and 3, using the strips and triangles from the B stack. This time, press the seams *away* from the triangles. Make 40, and label them Block B.

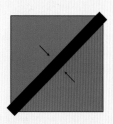

Make 40 of Block B.

 PLAN AHEAD! When you approach the bottom of the stack, lay out the triangle pairs so you have enough variety.

5. Place the bias line of a 6" square ruler on the center of the lattice strip. Square up the block to measure 4½". Repeat for all A and B blocks.

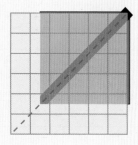

Assembling the Quilt Top

1. Arrange the blocks in 10 horizontal rows of 8 blocks each, alternating the A and B blocks and turning the blocks as shown in the quilt diagram below. Sew the blocks into rows. Press the seams in alternating directions from row to row. Sew the rows together; press.

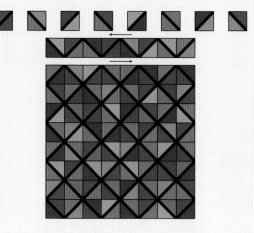

Quilt diagram

2. Refer to Squared Borders (page 17). Measure, trim, and sew borders to the top and bottom of the quilt. Press the seams toward the borders. Repeat to sew borders to the sides, piecing as necessary.

Finishing

Refer to Finishing Your Quilt (page 20).

1. Layer the quilt top, batting, and backing; baste.

2. Hand or machine quilt as desired.

3. Piece the 3" x 20" fat-quarter strips, and use them to bind the edges of the quilt.

4. Add a hanging sleeve and label if desired.

 REFLECT THE MOOD! *Asian Outlook* is quilted in an overall interlocking circle design, reflective of the traditional Japanese sashiko quilting pattern. Look for a quilting design that complements the theme or style of *your* quilt.

Quilt: *Tropical Reef*

Finished quilt: 50" x 72"

Finished block: 6" x 12"

Portuguese
Tiles

Tropical Reef, designed and made by M'Liss Rae Hawley,
machine quilted by Barbara Dau, 2003.

W hile looking at photos in one of my books about tiles, I came across a tiled wall in Lisbon, Portugal, dating from the first half of the seventeenth century. This was the inspiration for my pattern Portuguese Tiles. To maintain the integrity of the tile and recreate it in a quilt block, I enlarged the block to 6" x 12". Although this is an odd shape, I think it pays off in visual impact.

The pattern works best if you maintain high contrast between the background and foreground fabrics. Choose fat quarters that are substantially darker or lighter than the background selection. Because the blocks are elongated, the pieces are larger than those in many other patterns, making Portuguese Tiles a great showcase for interesting fabrics.

Materials

All yardage is based on 40"-wide fabric, unless otherwise stated.

8 fat quarters (variety of medium to dark value) for blocks

1¾ yards light fabric for block backgrounds

⅓ yard for inner border

1⅜ yards for outer border

4½ yards for backing

⅝ yard for binding

½ yard for hanging sleeve

58" x 80" piece of batting

Cutting

Cut along the 20" length of the fat quarters. Refer to What *is* a Fat Quarter? (page 8).

From *each* fat quarter:

Cut 5 strips, 3½" x 20"; crosscut into 8 rectangles, 3½" x 6½", and 8 squares, 3½" x 3½".

From the light background fabric:

Cut 17 strips, 3½" x 40"; crosscut into 64 rectangles, 3½" x 6½" and 64 squares, 3½" x 3½".

From the inner border fabric:

Cut 5 strips, 1½" x 40".

From the outer border fabric:

Cut 3 strips, 5½" x 40".

Cut 4 strips, 6½" x 40".

From the binding fabric:

Cut 7 strips, 3" x 40".

From the hanging sleeve fabric:

Cut 2 strips, 8½" x 40".

Portuguese Tile Blocks

1. Use a ruler and marking tool to draw a diagonal line from corner to corner on the wrong side of each 3½" square of fat-quarter and background fabric.

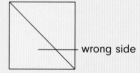

wrong side

2. With right sides together and raw edges aligned, place a 3½" background square on one end of each 3½" x 6½" fat-quarter rectangle, as shown. Sew directly on the diagonal line. Cut away the excess fabric, leaving a ¼" seam allowance. Press the seams toward the rectangle. Make 8 units in each color combination (64 units total), and label them unit A.

stitching line

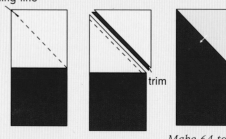

trim

Make 64 total of Unit A.

3. Repeat Step 2, placing a 3½" fat-quarter square on one end of each 3½" x 6½" background rectangle as shown. Press toward the square. Make 8 units in each color combination (64 units total), and label them unit B.

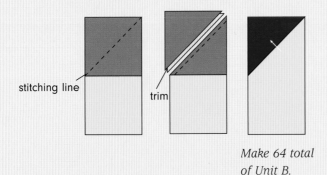

stitching line

trim

Make 64 total of Unit B.

4. Pair and sew matching-colored A and B units as shown; press. Make 32 of each (64 units total).

Make 32.   *Make 32.*

5. Sew 2 matching-colored units from Step 4 together as shown, matching the center seams; press. Make 4 blocks of each color combination (32 blocks total).

Make 32.

Assembling the Quilt Top

1. Lay out one of each block side by side in a pleasing color arrangement. Starting on the left, number and label the blocks 1 – 8.

2. Arrange the blocks in 5 horizontal rows of 6 blocks each, as shown in the quilt diagram. You will have 2

blocks left over. You may incorporate them into the label or the back of the quilt.

3. Sew the blocks into rows. Press the seams in alternating directions from row to row. Sew the rows together; press.

Quilt diagram

4. Refer to Squared Borders (page 17). Measure, trim, and sew an inner border strip to the top and bottom of the quilt. Press the seams toward the border. Repeat to sew inner borders to the sides, piecing as necessary.

5. Repeat Step 4 to sew the 5½" outer border strips to the top and bottom edges of the quilt, and the 6½" outer border strips to the sides, piecing as necessary. Press the seams toward the outer border.

Finishing

Refer to Finishing Your Quilt (page 20).

1. Piece the backing as described on page 20.

2. Layer the quilt top, batting, and backing; baste.

3. Hand or machine quilt as desired.

4. Use the 3"-wide strips to bind the edges of the quilt.

5. Add a hanging sleeve and label if desired.

London Roads

Quilt: *Stars Over London*

Finished quilt: 59" x 77"

Finished block: 3"

Stars Over London, designed and made by M'Liss Rae Hawley, machine quilted by Barbara Dau, 2003.

ondon Roads is a fast, fun, and easy pattern. The theme fabric sets the tone for the quilt, so this is a good place to start when selecting your fabric. The Fence Rail or "road" acts as an accent, while the four patches create a secondary pattern.

I love the way the pattern changes with different colorways, subject matter, and placement of fabric. This is an appealing choice for quilters of all skill levels.

Materials

All yardage is based on 40"-wide fabric, unless otherwise noted.

6 fat quarters (3 light and 3 medium values) for four-patch units

1⅜ yards of light fabric for fence-rail units

⅞ yard of theme fabric for squares

¾ yard medium fabric for fence-rail units

⅜ yard for inner border

1⅓ yards for outer border*

⅔ yard for binding

4¾ yards for backing

½ yard for hanging sleeve

68" x 85" piece of batting

*May be the same as the theme fabric.

Cutting

Cut along the 20" length of the fat quarters. Refer to What is a Fat Quarter? (page 8).

From each fat quarter:

Cut 7 strips, 2" x 20".

From the light fabric:

Cut 30 strips, 1½" x 40".

From the medium fabric:

Cut 15 strips, 1½" x 40".

From the theme fabric:

Cut 7 strips, 3½" x 40"; crosscut into 70 squares, 3½" x 3½".

From the inner border fabric:

Cut 6 strips, 1½" x 40".

From the outer border fabric:

Cut 6 strips, 6½" x 40".

From the binding fabric:

Cut 7 strips, 3" x 40".

From the hanging sleeve fabric:

Cut 2 strips, 8½" x 40".

tip | **REARRANGE FABRIC!** Not enough zip or "caffeine" in your design? Change the placement of value, and the "road" takes on another look. *Too Much or Not Enough Caffeine* (page 69) is an excellent example of the power of value in determining a quilt's design.

Four-Patch Units

1. Pair the light and medium value 2" x 20" strips into 3 color combinations. With right sides together, sew each pair of strips, making 21 strip sets total. Cut each strip set into segments 2" wide (210 segments total).

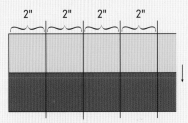

Make 21 strip sets. Cut 210 segments.

2. Stitch 2 matching segments together as shown; press. Make 104 four-patch units.

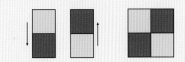

Make 104 total.

Fence-Rail Units

Sew a 1½" x 40" medium strip between two 1½" x 40" light strips to make a strip set; press. Make 15 strip sets. Crosscut into 157 segments, each 3½" wide.

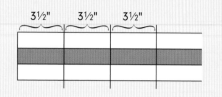

Make 15 strip sets. Cut 157 segments.

Assembling the Quilt Top

1. Arrange the four-patch units, the fence-rail units, and the 3½" theme fabric squares in 21 horizontal rows of 15 units and squares each, turning the units and squares as shown in the quilt diagram below. Sew into rows. Press the seams in alternating directions from row to row. Sew the rows together; press.

Quilt diagram

2. Refer to Squared Borders (page 17). Measure, trim, and sew an inner border strip to the top and bottom of the quilt top, piecing as necessary. Press the seams toward the border. Repeat to sew an inner border to the sides.

3. Arrange and sew four of the remaining four-patches as shown to make the corner squares; press. Make 4 corner squares.

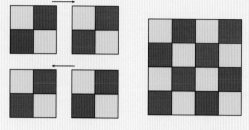

Make 4.

4. Refer to Borders with Corner Squares (page 17). Measure the quilt through the center from side to side and from top to bottom. Trim 2 outer border strips to each of these measurements, piecing as necessary.

5. Sew the shorter outer border strips to the top and bottom of the quilt. Press the seams toward the outer border. Sew a corner square from Step 3 to each end of the longer outer border strips. Press the seams toward the border strip. Sew to the sides of the quilt; press.

Finishing

Refer to Finishing Your Quilt (page 20).

1. Piece the backing as described on page 20.

2. Layer the quilt top, batting, and backing; baste.

3. Hand or machine quilt as desired.

4. Use the 3"-wide strips to bind the edges of the quilt.

5. Add a hanging sleeve and label if desired.

Quilt: *Lellow*

Finished quilt: 48¼" x 65½"

Embellished Braids

Lellow, designed, pieced, and embellished by M'Liss Rae Hawley, machine quilted by Barbara Dau, 2003.

Braids *is such a versatile pattern. I added embellishment and set the braid units in the coins configuration. This quilt is so much fun to make!*

When you select your fat quarters, keep in mind that the pattern requires 3 different colors or distinct values of fabric. For Lellow, *I selected two fat quarters each of white, gray, and black. The piecing process is much like braiding hair, with the fat-quarter fabrics labeled accordingly (1-2-3 and 4-5-6).*

For embellishment, I used white, black, and yellow rickrack and ribbons. The background is yellow, so Lellow *is a monochromatic, or one-color quilt.*

THINK FLANNEL! Embellished Braids is a wonderful pattern for using cuddly flannel fabrics.

Materials

All yardage is based on 40"-wide fabric, unless otherwise noted.

6 fat quarters (2 *each* of 3 different colors) for braids

1½ yards for background

1⅛ yards for border

⅝ yard for binding

4⅛ yards for backing

½ yard for hanging sleeve

57" x 74" piece of batting

2 yards 20"-wide medium-weight tear-away stabilizer

Embellishments, such as coordinating colors of rickrack (in a variety of widths) and grosgrain and satin ribbon (⅛"–¼" wide)

Cutting

Cut along the 20" length of the fat quarters. Refer to What *is* a Fat Quarter? (page 8).

From *each* fat quarter:

Cut 6 strips, 2½" x 20"; cut 3 strips of each fat quarter into 12 rectangles, 2½" x 4¾" (72 rectangles total).

From the *length* of the background fabric:

Cut 5 strips, 4¾" x 47½".

Cut 2 strips, 4¾" x 38¾".

From the border fabric:

Cut 6 strips, 5½" x 40".

From the binding fabric:

Cut 6 strips, 3" x 40".

From the hanging sleeve fabric:

Cut 2 strips, 8½" x 40".

From the stabilizer:

Cut 3 pieces, 20" x 22".

GREAT FINDS! Garage and estate sales, thrift stores, and flea markets often yield funky vintage trims and fabulous antique laces.

Embellished–Braid Units

1. Lay one 2" x 20" strip of each fat-quarter fabric face up on a piece of stabilizer; pin. Cut the various rickrack, ribbons, and trims into 22" lengths. Place one on each strip, allowing for a ¼" seam allowance on both of the strip's long edges. Stitch the embellishments to the strips. Make 3 stabilized pieces with 6 strips each.

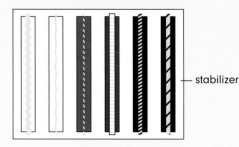

— stabilizer

Make 3.

2. Press the strips on the right side and remove the stabilizer. Square up the ends of each embellished strip as necessary and crosscut into 4 rectangles, 2½" x 4¾" (72 rectangles total).

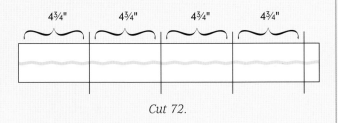

Cut 72.

3. Stack the rectangles by fat-quarter fabric and label the stacks 1–6, mixing the plain and embellished rectangles together in each stack.

4. Each of the 4 embellished-braid units is made from 36 rectangles: 6 of each fat-quarter fabric. The order of the fabrics in each unit follows the numbered sequence, mixing the pieced and embellished rectangles randomly. **The order never changes—just the fabric you start with.**

The units are built from bottom to top. Unit 1 (far left) begins with fabric 1; Unit 2 begins with fabric 2; Unit 3 begins with fabric 5; and Unit 4 (far right) begins with fabric 6.

5. To make Unit 1, place a fabric 1 and a fabric 2 rectangle at a 90° angle, and sew them together along the top edge as shown. Do not press yet; you will press when the entire unit is sewn.

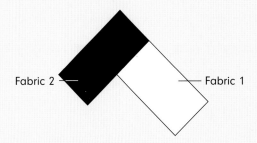

6. Sew the next (fabric 3) rectangle to the side of the unit from Step 5 as shown.

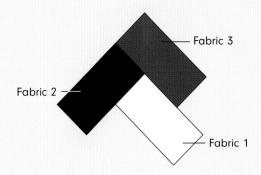

7. Repeat Steps 5 and 6 until you have sewn 36 rectangles in numeric sequence to complete Unit 1.

Unit 1

8. Gently press the unit on the back, from bottom to top. Press the first seam toward the bottom of the unit and the rest of the seams toward the top. Next, press the unit on the front, also from bottom to top. Spray with sizing or starch, press.

9. Stay-stitch just inside (1/8"–3/16") the side edges of the unit as shown. Use a rotary cutter to trim *just outside* the stay stitching so the unit measures 4¾" wide.

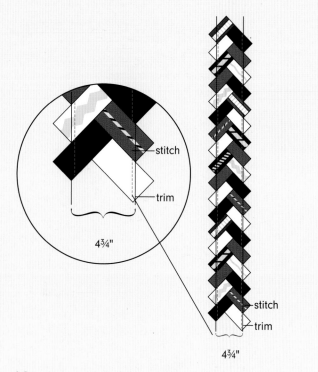

10. Beginning with fabric 2 and keeping the fabrics in numeric order, repeat Steps 5–9 to construct Unit 2.

Unit 2. Begin with fabric 2.

11. Repeat Steps 5–9 to construct Units 3 and 4 as shown. Begin Unit 3 with fabric 5 and Unit 4 with fabric 6.

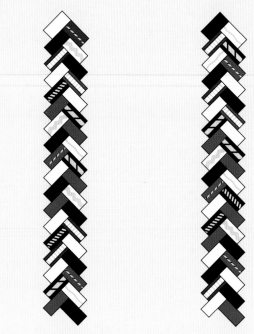

Unit 3. Begin with fabric 5.   *Unit 4. Begin with fabric 6.*

12. Trim each braid unit along the top edge first, being sure to preserve the point at the top of each braid and allowing a ¼" seam allowance. Trim the bottom edges so that each braid measures 47½" long. Stay-stitch the top and bottom edge of each unit.

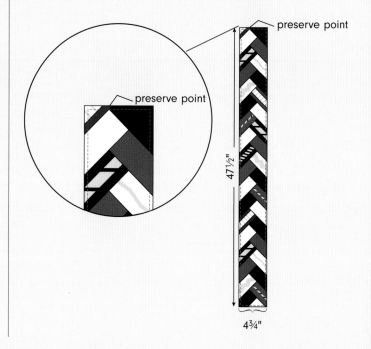

Assembling the Quilt Top

1. Arrange Units 1–4 and the 4¾" x 47½" background strips, alternating them as shown in the quilt diagram below. Sew the units and strips together. Press the seams toward the background strips. Sew the 4¾" x 38¾" background strips to the top and bottom edges; press.

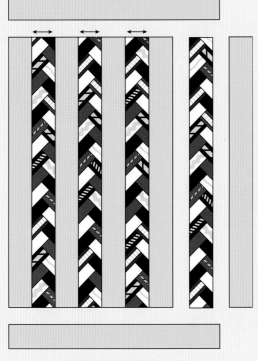

Quilt diagram

2. Refer to Squared Borders (page 17). Measure, trim, and sew a border strip to the top and bottom of the quilt, piecing as necessary. Press the seams toward the border. Repeat to sew borders to the sides; press.

Finishing

Refer to Finishing Your Quilt (page 20).

1. Piece the backing as described on page 20.

2. Layer the quilt top, batting, and backing; baste.

3. Hand or machine quilt as desired.

4. Use the 3"-wide strips to bind the edges of the quilt.

5. Add a hanging sleeve and label if desired.

Vicki DeGraaf makes excellent use of lace and other delicate embellishments in her quilt Lacey Braids. *For a full view of this quilt, see page 71.*

Serendipity

Quilt: *Serendipity*

Finished quilt: 42⅜" x 52¼"

Finished block: 7"

Serendipity, designed and made by M'Liss Rae Hawley,
machine quilted by Barbara Dau, 2003.

You are going to adore making this quilt! *Serendipity* is a fast and fun pattern, and the perfect size for a wallhanging or a baby quilt. The blocks are set on point with three different background (or setting) fabrics. This makes the quilt more interesting, without increasing the degree of difficulty.

The frog fabric in the border of my quilt literally fell off the shelf, and I found the six fat quarters in my fabric collection in record time. For the background, I envisioned a medium value of yellow-green (or chartreuse) and found three that worked perfectly. Considering the ease with which I designed the pattern and selected the fabric, I had no choice but to call both the pattern and my quilt Serendipity!

Materials

All yardage is based on 40"-wide fabric, unless otherwise stated.

6 fat quarters (2 each of light, medium, and dark value) for blocks

3/8 yard *each* of 3 similar fabrics for block centers and setting triangles

1/4 yard for inner border

1 yard for outer border

5/8 yard for binding

3 1/2 yards for backing

1/2 yard for hanging sleeve

52" x 62" piece of batting

Cutting

Cut along the 20" length of the fat quarters. Refer to What *is* a Fat Quarter? (page 8).

From *each* of the 2 light-value fat quarters:
Cut 9 strips, 1 1/4" x 20".

From *each* of the 2 medium-value fat quarters:
Cut 9 strips, 1 1/2" x 20".

From *each* of the 2 dark-value fat quarters:
Cut 9 strips, 1 3/4" x 20".

From 3/8 yard #1:
Cut 1 square, 12 1/2" x 12 1/2"; crosscut twice diagonally to yield 4 quarter-square side setting triangles.

Cut 1 square, 10" x 10"; crosscut once diagonally to yield 2 half-square corner setting triangles.

Cut 6 squares, 1 1/2" x 1 1/2".

From 3/8 yard #2:
Cut 1 square, 12 1/2" x 12 1/2"; crosscut twice diagonally to yield 4 quarter-square side setting triangles.

Cut 6 squares, 1 1/2" x 1 1/2".

From 3/8 yard #3:
Cut 1 square, 12 1/2" x 12 1/2"; crosscut twice diagonally to yield 4 quarter-square side setting triangles

Cut 1 square 10" x 10"; crosscut once diagonally to yield 2 half-square corner setting triangles.

Cut 6 squares, 1 1/2" x 1 1/2".

From the inner border fabric:
Cut 5 strips, 1 1/8" x 40".

From the outer border fabric:
Cut 5 strips, 5 1/2" x 40".

From the binding fabric:
Cut 6 strips, 3" x 40".

From the hanging sleeve fabric:
Cut 2 strips, 8 1/2" x 40".

Serendipity Blocks

You will need 18 Serendipity blocks for this quilt: 12 of Block 1 and 6 of Block 2.

1. Separate the fat-quarter strips into 2 groups, each containing a light, medium, and dark value. Label the groups A and B.

2. Using the group A strips, sew the 1½" medium-value strip between the 1¼" light-value strip and the 1¾" dark-value strip to make a strip set as shown below. Press the seams toward the light fabric. Make 9 strip sets. Crosscut 36 segments total, 4½" wide, and label the segments A.

3. Repeat Step 2, using the group B strips and labeling the segments B.

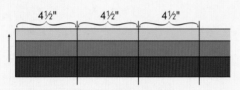

Make 9 A and 9 B strip sets (18 total).
Cut 36 A and 36 B segments.

4. Sort the segments from Step 2 and Step 3 into 18 stacks: 2 A and 2 B segments per stack. Add a 1½" center square to each stack.

5. Working one stack at a time, arrange a center square and the 2 A and 2 B segments as shown.

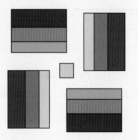

6. With right sides together, sew the center square to the upper right edge of the first segment, stopping halfway with a backstitch to make a partial seam.

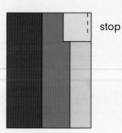

7. Sew the remaining segments around the center square in the order shown.

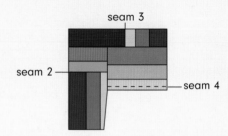

8. Complete the partial seam between the first segment and the center square. Press the seams away from the center square. Make 12 blocks and label them Block 1.

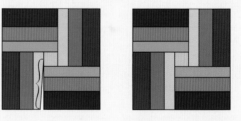

Make 12 of Block 1.

9. Repeat Steps 5 through 8, arranging the A and B segments as shown. Make 6 blocks and label them Block 2.

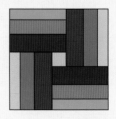

Make 6 of Block 2.

Assembling the Quilt Top

The side and corner triangles are cut oversized so the blocks appear to float. You will square up the quilt top after it is assembled.

1. Arrange the blocks and setting triangles in diagonal rows, alternating Block 1 and Block 2 as shown in the quilt diagram below. You will have two side setting triangles left over.

2. Sew the blocks together in diagonal rows. Press the seams in alternating directions from row to row. Add the *side* setting triangles. Press the seams toward the triangles. (You'll sew the corner setting triangles in the next step.)

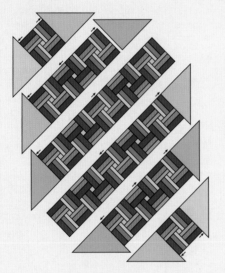

Quilt diagram

3. Sew the rows together; press. Trim the "dog ears" at each corner shown. Sew the corner setting triangles to the quilt. Press the seams toward the triangles.

4. Square up the quilt top, measuring 1" from the points of the blocks to trim the side and corner triangles.

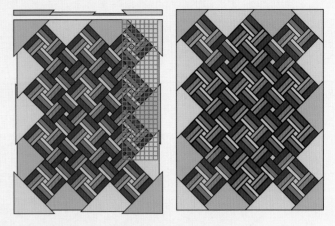

Trim triangles 1" from block points.

5. With right sides together and long raw edges aligned, sew 1⅛"-wide inner border strips and 5½"-wide outer border strips together in pairs. Refer to Mitered Borders (page 19) to measure, fit, and sew the border units to the quilt, piecing as necessary. Miter the corners. Press the seams toward the borders.

Finishing

Refer to Finishing Your Quilt (page 20).

1. Piece the backing as described on page 20.

2. Layer the quilt top, batting, and backing; baste.

3. Hand or machine quilt as desired.

4. Use the 3"-wide strips to bind the edges of the quilt.

5. Add a hanging sleeve and label if desired.

Millennium

Circles of Life, designed and made by M'Liss Rae Hawley, machine quilted by M'Liss Rae Hawley and Barbara Dau, 2003.

Our world, a sphere, is full of circles. Circles are powerful symbols used throughout the ages in architecture, art, and religion. Examples include the calendar stones of the Aztecs, Hawaiian Menehune rings, Native American medicine wheels, and the wedding ring. Mandala is the Sanskrit word for circle.

The Millennium pattern places quarter circles in two opposing corners of the traditional Fence Rail block. To get the full effect, you will need to select two different values of the same color for the quarter circles. Half the blocks feature the darker fabric, and the remaining half, the lighter value. Give it a try; the effect is well worth the effort!

Materials

Yardage is based on 40"-wide fabric, unless otherwise noted.

6 fat quarters for fence rails (piece A)

2 fat quarters in the same color (1 light, 1 darker) for quarter circles (piece B)

¼ yard for inner border

1 yard for outer border

½ yard for binding

2⅞ yards for backing

½ yard for hanging sleeve

50" x 56" piece of batting

Cutting

Cut along the 20" length of fat quarters. Refer to What *is* a Fat Quarter? (page 8). Use the pattern on page 53 to make a template to cut piece B.

From *each* fat-quarter fence-rail fabric:
Cut 10 strips, 1½" x 20".

From *each* fat-quarter quarter-circle fabric:
Cut 30 of piece B.

From the inner border fabric:
Cut 4 strips, 1¼" x 40".

From the outer border fabric:
Cut 5 strips, 5¾" x 40".

From the binding fabric:
Cut 5 strips, 3" x 40".

From the hanging sleeve fabric:
Cut 2 strips, 8½" x 40".

CIRCLES! Yes, I think all quilters should make at least one quilt with pieced circles. Think of it this way: it's like setting in sleeves on Barbie doll dresses!

cir • cle:

1. a plane figure bonded by a single curved line, called its circumference, every point of which is equally distant from a point at the center of the figure: all lines drawn from the center to the circumference, or periphery, are equal to each other.

2. a group of people bound together by a common interest; a coterie; as, a circle of friends.

Webster's *New Twentieth Century Dictionary,* Unabridged

Millennium Blocks

1. Arrange 1 of each color 1½"-wide fat-quarter strips in the order you prefer. (Note that fabrics 1 and 6 will create a continuing fence rail if they are dominating colors.) Sew the strips together, and press the seams in one direction. Make 10 identical strip sets. Crosscut into 30 segments, each 6½".

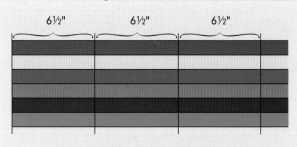

Make 10 strip sets. Cut 30 segments.

2. Use the pattern on page 53 to make a template for piece A. Position the template over each 6½" segment from Step 1, aligning the upper right and lower left corners. Use a pencil to trace the two curves on the opposite corners. Cut on the drawn lines; save the cut-away curved pieces for another project.

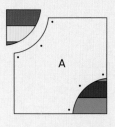

3. Clip along the curve of each A piece, taking care to stay well within the seam allowance. *Do not cut beyond the seam line.* Mark matchpoints on the curved edges of each A piece and on all light and dark B pieces.

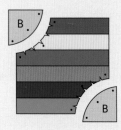

4. With right sides together and aligning the matchpoints, gently ease and pin the curved edges of an A piece with a light-colored B piece. With B on top, stitch the curve. Repeat in the opposite corner to complete the block. Press the seam away from B. Make 15 blocks and label them Block 1.

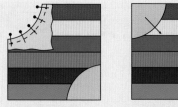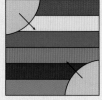

Make 15 of Block 1.

5. Repeat Step 4, using the remaining A pieces and the darker-colored B pieces. Make 15 blocks and label them Block 2.

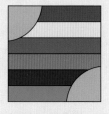

Make 15 of Block 2.

Assembling the Quilt Top

1. Arrange the blocks in 6 horizontal rows of 5 blocks each, alternating and rotating the Blocks 1 and 2 as shown in the quilt diagram below. Sew the blocks into rows. Press the seams in alternating directions from row to row. Sew the rows together; press.

Quilt diagram

2. Refer to Squared Borders (page 17). Measure, trim, and sew an inner border strip to the top and bottom of the quilt. Press the seams toward the border. Repeat to sew inner borders to the sides; press.

3. Repeat Step 2 to measure, trim, and sew the outer borders to the quilt, piecing as necessary. Press the seams toward the outer borders.

Finishing

Refer to Finishing Your Quilt (page 20).

1. Piece the backing as described on page 20.

2. Layer the quilt top, batting, and backing; baste.

3. Hand or machine quilt as desired.

4. Use the 3"-wide strips to bind the edges of the quilt.

5. Add a hanging sleeve and label if desired.

tip **BUTTONS!** New, used, recycled, or antique; don't overlook this sewing-box standby as a wonderful source of embellishment. Hunt for interesting shapes or novelty pieces to complement your fabrics or theme.

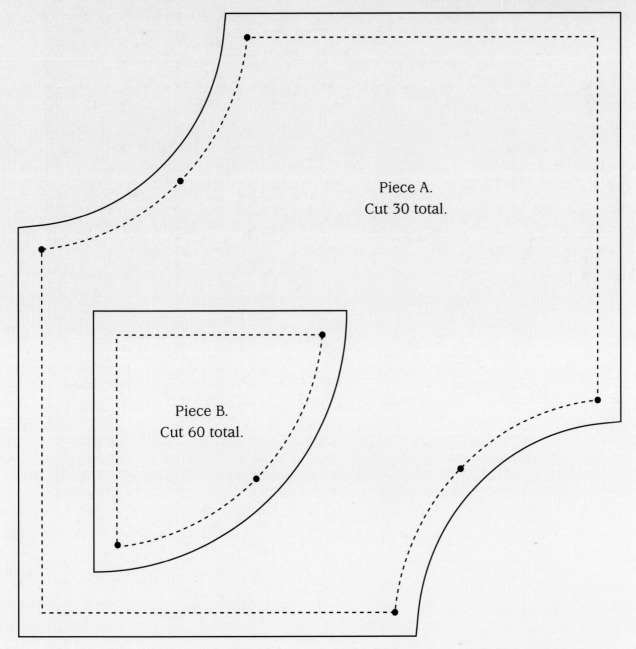

Piece A.
Cut 30 total.

Piece B.
Cut 60 total.

Windows

Quilt: *Spring View Through Rose-Colored Glasses*

Finished quilt: 49½" x 49½"

Finished block: 7½"

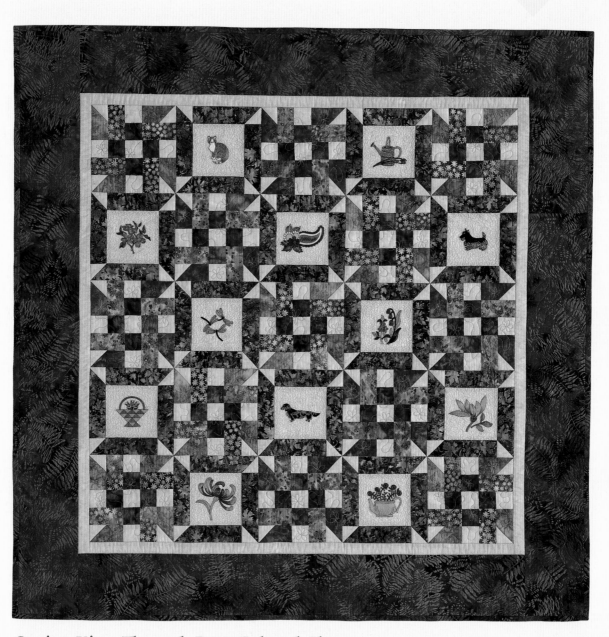

Spring View Through Rose-Colored Glasses, designed and made by
M'Liss Rae Hawley, machine quilted by Barbara Dau, 2003.

I fell in love with machine embroideries the first time I saw them and decided one day I would design my own collections. Once I had done that, designing coordinating fabric was a natural. Next came the quilt patterns to showcase both the embroideries and the fabric.

Windows, the pattern I designed, is unique in that the embroideries are framed as individual blocks. Although each pieced block is separate and stands alone, a pinwheel is created when four blocks come together—an added bonus! I hope you enjoy creating your own embroidery-filled "windows."

Materials

All yardage is based on 40"-wide fabric, unless otherwise stated.

5 fat quarters for pieced blocks *

1½ yards for embroidered and pieced-block backgrounds

½ yard for embroidered block frames

¼ yard for inner border

1 yard for outer border

⅝ yard for binding

3¼ yards for backing

½ yard for hanging sleeve

58" x 58" piece of batting

Fabric stabilizer (See Machine Embroidery Tips, page 18.)

Embroidery card(s) of your choice
(See Resources, page 80.)

Rayon embroidery threads in assorted colors

This pattern uses just 5 fat quarters, so if you are working with a packet of 6, set one aside for another project.

Use rayon threads in assorted colors for your embroideries.

Cutting

Cut along the 20" length of the fat quarters. Refer to What *is* a Fat Quarter? (page 8).

From *each* of fat quarters 1 and 2:
Cut 6 strips, 2" x 20"; crosscut into 28 rectangles, 2" x 3½" (56 rectangles total).

From fat quarter 3:
Cut 6 strips, 2" x 20".

From *each* of fat quarters 4 and 5:
Cut 6 strips, 2" x 20"; crosscut into 28 rectangles, 2" x 3½" (56 rectangles total).

From the background fabric:
Cut 9 strips, 2" x 40"; crosscut 3 strips into 6 strips, 2" x 20". Crosscut the remaining strips into 104 squares, 2" x 2".

Cut 3 strips, 9½" x 40"; crosscut into 12 squares, 9½" x 9½".*

From the embroidered block frame fabric:
Cut 8 strips, 2" x 40"; crosscut into 48 rectangles, 2" x 6½".

From the inner border fabric:
Cut 4 strips, 1½" x 40".

From the outer border fabric:
Cut 5 strips, 5½" x 40".

From the binding fabric:
Cut 6 strips, 3" x 40".

From the hanging sleeve fabric:
Cut 2 strips, 8½" x 40".

Adjust as needed to fit your embroidery hoop.

DOUBLE DUTY! When you are planning to alternate two different blocks in your quilt, look for ways to adapt the block corners to create secondary designs where the blocks meet. The alternating blocks in the Windows pattern are a good example. By introducing small triangles to the corner of each block, tiny pinwheels appear!

Detail of block corners on Spring View Through Rose-Colored Glasses *(page 54).*

Embroidered Blocks

1. Stabilize each 9½" background square following the manufacturer's instructions. Select an embroidery collection and embroider a different motif in each square. Trim the embroidered squares to 5" x 5". Cut the squares to best suit the embroidery design; do not worry about the grain of the fabric.

2. Use a ruler and marking tool to draw a diagonal line from corner to corner on the wrong side of a 2" background square. Mark 48 squares.

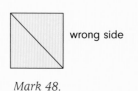

wrong side

Mark 48.

3. With right sides together and raw edges aligned, place a 2" background square on one end of each 2" x 6½" block frame rectangle, as shown. Sew directly on the diagonal line. Cut away the excess fabric, leaving a ¼" seam allowance. Press toward the square. Make 48 units.

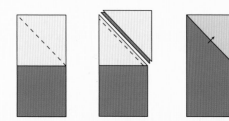

Make 48.

4. Sew a unit from Step 3 to the top of an embroidered square, beginning in the upper left corner as shown. Stop stitching 2½" from the upper right corner with a backstitch to make a partial seam.

Stop and backstitch.

5. Sew the remaining units to the embroidered square in the order shown. Complete the partial seam between the first unit and the embroidered square. Press all the seams away from the embroidered square. Make 12 blocks.

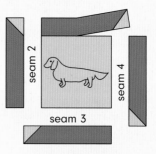

seam 2
seam 4
seam 3

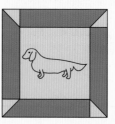

Make 12.

TELL A STORY! Windows is a great pattern to tell your story. In her quilt *Frog Frolic* (page 77), Anastasia Riordan used her embroidery patterns to tell the tale of how men and women prepare for a date . . . all from a frog's point of view!

Choose from a wide selection of embroidery collections to tell your story.

Pieced Blocks

1. Repeat Steps 2 and 3 of Embroidered Blocks (page 56) using the 2" background squares and 2" x 3½" fat quarter 1 and 2 rectangles. Make 56 units.

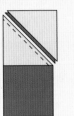

Make 56.

2. With right sides together, sew a 2" x 20" background strip and a 2" x 20" fat quarter 3 strip together to make a strip set. Press toward the dark fabric. Make 6 strip sets. Crosscut the strip sets into 56 segments, each 2" wide.

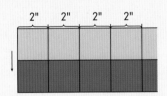

Make 6 strip sets. Cut 56 segments.

 IT'S SO EASY! Use a 5" ruler to trim the embroidery square, or tape off a 5" square on a larger ruler. Center the motif in the 5" square and trim the first two sides. Turn the ruler, aligning the ruler's edge with the previously cut edge of the fabric square, and trim the remaining two sides of the square.

 BE CREATIVE! If you don't own or have access to an amazing embroidery machine, fill the windows with your individual story . . . told in appliqué.

3. Arrange 4 matching units from Step 1, 4 matching 2" x 3½" fat quarter 4 and 5 rectangles, 4 strip-set segments from Step 2, and a remaining 2" background square in 3 rows, as shown. Sew the units and pieces into rows; press. Sew the rows together; press. Make 7 blocks in each color combination (14 blocks total).

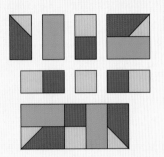
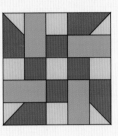

Make 7.

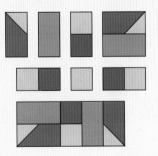
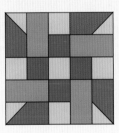

Make 7.

Assembling the Quilt Top

Note: The quilt requires 13 pieced blocks. When you decide on the block layout, you may incorporate the leftover block into the back of the quilt, or use it in the label.

1. Arrange the blocks in 5 horizontal rows of 5 blocks each as shown in the quilt diagram below. Sew the blocks into rows. Press the seams in alternating directions from row to row. Sew the rows together; press.

2. Refer to Squared Borders (page 17). Measure, trim, and sew an inner border strip to the top and bottom of the quilt. Press the seams toward the border. Repeat to sew inner borders to the sides, piecing as necessary.

3. Repeat Step 2 to measure, trim, and sew the outer borders to the quilt, piecing as necessary. Press the seams toward the outer borders.

Finishing

Refer to Finishing Your Quilt (page 20).

1. Piece the backing as described on page 20.

2. Layer the quilt top, batting, and backing; baste.

3. Hand or machine quilt as desired.

4. Use the 3"-wide strips to bind the edges of the quilt.

5. Add a hanging sleeve and label if desired.

tip **STIPPLE QUILTING!** When you fill the background with quilting, the foreground motif becomes more prominent. What a wonderful way to make those embroideries pop!

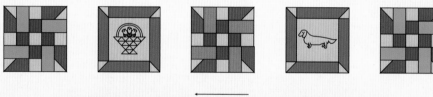

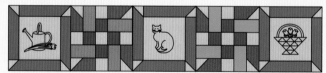

Quilt diagram

Blowing in the Wind

51" x 64", designed and made by M'Liss Rae Hawley,
machine quilted by Barbara Dau, 2003.

Pinwheels pattern (page 28).

Happiness

51" x 64", made by Barbara Higbee-Price,
machine quilted by Barbara Dau, 2003.

Pinwheels pattern (page 28).

Jumpin' Jack Flash

50" x 63", made by Carla Zimmerman,
machine quilted by Al and Shelly Withall, 2003.

Pinwheels pattern (page 28).

Double Dutch

51" x 64", made by Anastasia Riordan, machine quilted by Pamela Uhlig, 2003.

Pinwheels pattern (page 28).

Spin: From Africa

45" x 54", made and hand quilted by Lucia G. T. Pan, 2003.

Pinwheels pattern (page 28).

A Thousand Wishes
50" x 62¼", made by Susie Kincy,
machine quilted by Barbara Dau, 2003.

Pinwheels pattern (page 28).

Christmas Interrupted
38" x 46", made by Vicki DeGraaf,
machine quilted by Barbara Dau, 2003.

Quilt Interrupted pattern (page 32).

Life is Like a Box of Chocolates
38" x 46", made by Anastasia Riordan,
machine quilted by Barbara Dau, 2003.

Quilt Interrupted pattern (page 32).

Aged to Perfection
40½" x 48¼", made by Susie Kincy,
machine quilted by Barbara Dau, 2003.

Quilt Interrupted pattern (page 32).

Technicolor Hugs and Kisses
38" x 46", made and quilted by
Carla Zimmerman, 2003.

Quilt Interrupted pattern (page 32).

Purple Dreams
50" x 72", made by Barbara Higbee-Price,
machine quilted by Doris Ellis, 2003.

Portuguese Tiles pattern (page 35).

Iznik
50" x 72", made and quilted
by Tim Canan, 2003.

Portuguese Tiles pattern (page 35).

Fall Harvest
50" x 72", designed and made by
M'Liss Rae Hawley, machine quilted
by Barbara Dau, 2003.

Portuguese Tiles pattern (page 35).

African Tiles

50" x 72", made by Annette Barca,
machine quilted by Barbara Dau, 2003.

Portuguese Tiles pattern (page 35).

Epiphany

57½" x 55", made by Anastasia Riordan,
machine quilted by Barbara Dau, 2003.

Portuguese Tiles pattern (page 35).

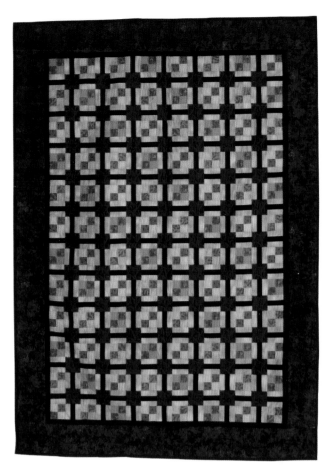

The Irish Road to London
59" x 72", made by Erin Rae Frandsen,
machine quilted by Barbara Dau, 2003.

London Roads pattern (page 38).

Spring in London
59½" x 77", made by Anastasia Riordan,
machine quilted by Pamela Uhlig, 2003.

London Roads pattern (page 38).

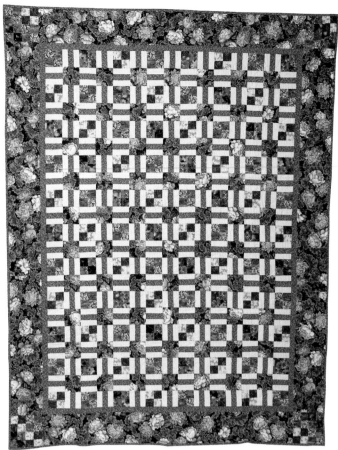

Peonies on Parade
59" x 72", made by Vicki DeGraaf,
machine quilted by Doris Ellis, 2003.

London Roads pattern (page 38).

Bowser Alley
59" x 72", made by Bev Green,
machine quilted by Barbara Dau, 2003.

London Roads pattern (page 38).

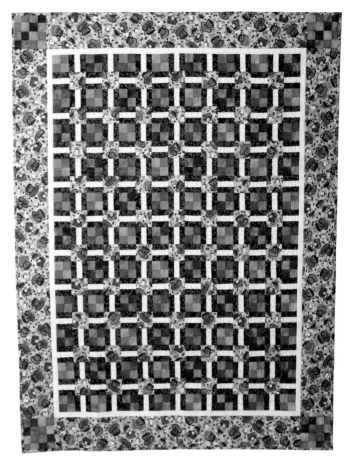

Too Much or Not Enough Caffeine
59" x 71", made by Peggy Johnson,
machine quilted by Barbara Dau, 2003.

London Roads pattern (page 38).

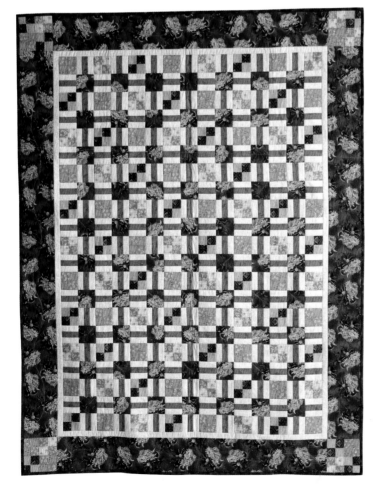

My English Garden
57½" x 79", made by Susie Kincy,
machine quilted by Barbara Dau, 2003.

London Roads pattern (page 38).

Stars and Stripes
54" x 61", made by Erin Rae Frandsen, machine quilted by Barbara Dau, 2003.

Embellished Braids pattern (page 41).

Zoya's Tea Party
54" x 61", made by Anastasia Riordan, machine quilted by Barbara Dau, 2003.

Embellished Braids pattern (page 41).

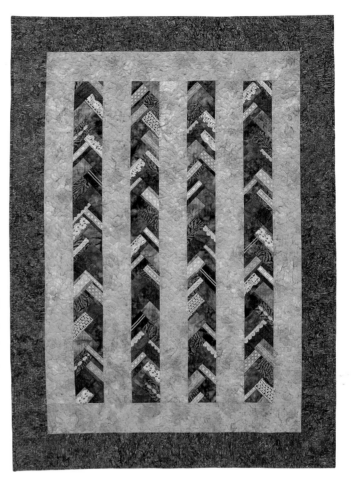

Lacey Braids

54" x 61", made by Vicki DeGraaf,
machine quilted by Doris Ellis, 2003.

Embellished Braids pattern (page 41).

It's a Guy Thing

50⅜" x 67⅜", made by Susie Kincy,
machine quilted by Barbara Dau, 2003.

Embellished Braids pattern (page 41).

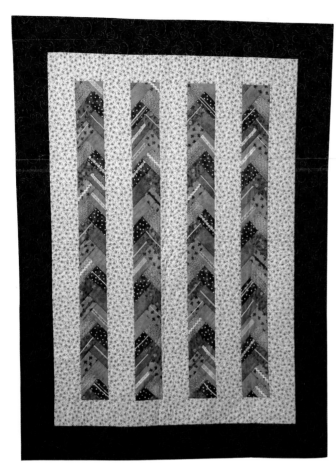

Sweet and Fun with a Little Bit of Fancy
54" x 61", made and machine quilted
by Suzanne Neil, 2003.

Embellished Braids pattern (page 41).

Stepping Stones to My Garden
42" x 52", made and machine quilted
by Stacie Johnson, 2003.

Serendipity pattern (page 46).

Paris Fashion

45" x 54⅜", made by Susie Kincy, machine quilted by Barbara Dau, 2003.

Serendipity pattern (page 46).

Wired on Double Shots

42" x 52", made by John and Louise James, machine quilted by Shelly Withall, 2003.

Serendipity pattern (page 46).

Fall's Festival

42" x 52", made by Annette Barca, machine quilted by Barbara Dau, 2003.

Serendipity pattern (page 46)

Cosmic Order

42" x 42", designed and made by M'Liss Rae Hawley,
machine quilted by Barbara Dau, 2003.

Millennium pattern (page 50).

Meet Me at the Corner of Hope and Love
42" x 48", made by Carla Zimmerman, machine quilted by Al and Shelly Withall, 2003.

Millennium pattern (page 50).

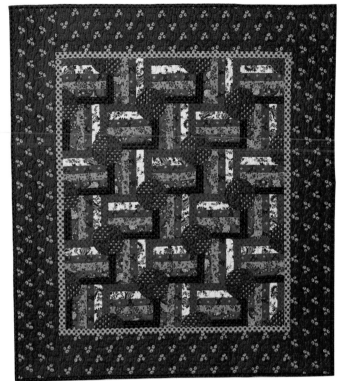

Many Moons Ago
42" x 48", made by John and Louise James, machine quilted by Al and Shelly Withall, 2003.

Millennium pattern (page 50).

Frog Frolic

48½" x 48½", made by Anastasia Riordan,
machine quilted by Barbara Dau, 2003.

Windows pattern (page 54).

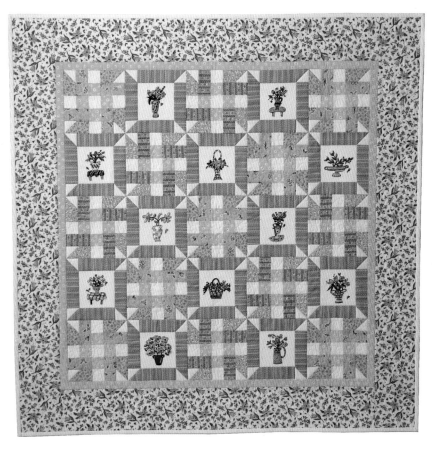

My Favorite Flowers

49½" x 49¾", made by Susie Kincy,
machine quilted by Barbara Dau, 2003.

Windows pattern (page 54).

Autumn View on Whidbey Island

49½" x 49½", designed and made by M'Liss Rae Hawley,
machine quilted by Barbara Dau, 2003.

Windows pattern (page 54).

Quilts in a Quilt
49½" x 49½", made by Barbara
Higbee-Price, machine quilted by
Barbara Dau, 2003.
Windows pattern (page 54).

Index

Resources

Cotton Patch Mail Order
3405 Hall Lane, Dept, CTB
Lafayette, CA 94549
Phone: 1-800-835-4418
Email: quiltusa@yahoo.com
Web: www.quiltusa.com

FAT-QUARTER PACKETS MAIL ORDER:
In The Beginning
8201 Lake City Way N.E.
Seattle, WA 98115
(206)523-8862

Connecting Threads
13118 N.E. 4th St.
Vancouver, WA 98684
(800) 574-6454
www.connectingthreads.com

Keepsake Quilting
P.O. Box 1618
Center Harbor, NH 03226
(800) 865-9458
www.keepsakequilting.com

INTERNET:
Big Horn Quilts
PO Box 566
Greybull, WY 82426
(877) 586-9150
www.bighornquilts.com

EMBROIDERY COLLECTIONS
These embroidery collections and more
are available at your local participating
Husqvarna Viking and Pfaff dealer.

The Big Easy (page 28)
Mardi Gras, EZ Sew Designs, Disk Part
#756 101300, multiformat CD-ROM
Cactus Punch, Holidays & Events, Volume
4, Mardi Gras Masks, HE04

Spring View Through Rose-Colored
Glasses (page 54) Spring View, by M'Liss
Rae Hawley, Disk Part #756 255100,
multi-format CD-ROM

Autumn View on Whidbey Island
(page 78) My Favorite Quilt Designs,
by M'Liss Rae Hawley, Disk Part #756
253300, multi-format CD-ROM

My Favorite Flowers (page 77)
Special Arrangements, by Marna Hill,
Disk Part #756 253400, multi-format
CD-ROM

Quilts in a Quilt (page 79)
My Favorite Quilt Designs, Disk Part #756
253300 and Spring View, Disk Part #756
255100, multi-format CD-ROM, both by
M'Liss Rae Hawley.

Frog Frolic (page 77)
Frog Fun, by Mary Lou Yetman, Disk Part
#756 255200, multi-format CD-ROM

About the Author

M'Liss Rae Hawley is an accomplished quilting teacher, lecturer, embroidery and textile designer, and best-selling author. She conducts workshops and seminars throughout North America. As the author of four books and the originator of numerous innovative designs, M'Liss is constantly seeking new boundaries to challenge her students while imparting her enthusiasm and love for the art of quilting.

Although she is in production for her new PBS television series, *M'Liss's World of Quilts,* M'Liss continues to design fabric with coordinating embroidery collections, write books, and create patterns for *McCall's Quilting* magazine. She likes to break quilting down to the basics to show students that quilting can be easy and fun at any level of skill!

M'Liss and her husband, Michael, live on Whidbey Island, Washington, in a filbert orchard. Michael is the sheriff of Island County, as well as a best-selling author. Their son is in the Marine Corps, and their daughter is in college. Michael and M'Liss share their home with five dachshunds and three cats.